It's Okay to Feel Crazy Trying to Have a Baby

Dalya Shaw

BALBOA.
PRESS
A DIVISION OF HAY HOUSE

Balboa Press books may be ordered through booksellers or by contacting:

Balboa Press
A Division of Hay House
1663 Liberty Drive
Bloomington, IN 47403
www.balboapress.com.au
1 (877) 407-4847

Print information available on the last page.

ISBN: 978-1-5043-1328-5 (sc)
ISBN: 978-1-5043-1329-2 (e)

Balboa Press rev. date: 06/21/2018

Contents

Dedication

To my beautiful and wonderful son and my best friend. You have brought me so much joy, in a few short years, and taught me so much. I could not want for a better relationship than what we have, and I feel so blessed to be your mum.

I wish for you to experience all life has to offer, regret nothing and most of all, find your purpose, follow your soul and always live with love in your life.

I am so very proud of you and will love you always …

Foreword

So, you want to have a baby? And it's making you feel crazy?

I smile as I write this as I know *exactly* how you feel. I felt the same way. For me, it started out as a want and then turned into a need, and towards the end, could have been described as an obsession. I have tried pretty much everything from artificial insemination, several full IVF cycles and even donor sperm and spent a huge amount of money in the process. So, I get it. I know how tough it is and I know how much you want this.

As I went on my baby making journey and spoke with numerous other women who were trying to fall pregnant or who had lost babies through miscarriage, it became evident to me, that a lot of our emotions were the same. A lot of what we were feeling was at times so incredibly intense and so unbelievably painful that no amount of theory, logic, comfort or encouragement could have changed what was going on inside our heads. This 'thinking' was probably part of the problem, and even today, I still don't really see a definitive way of changing that as it is based on emotion.

For me, I felt the longer it took to fall pregnant, the less people I wanted to tell what we were doing, and the less people we associated with. I couldn't bear the "*are you pregnant yet*?" or "*how's it all going*?" questions that came every couple of weeks.

You get to the point that you just wish you were invisible and wish you had never said anything to anyone in the first place. They cannot understand what you are going through unless they have been there themselves, and at times you end up trying to make them feel more comfortable if they have asked a question that, unbeknownst to them, is another devastating reminder and never a good time. Yes, I have been there too. It is a no-win situation for an outsider trying to help and no amount of empathy makes what you are going through mentally and physically feel okay.

So, to all women out there! To all women who are embarking on a journey of trying to have what we have been told for thousands of years is our 'rite of passage' to have a beautiful and healthy child, this book is for you.

For all the men out there, that are trying to comprehend what a woman is going through, and what kind of thoughts are flying around her head, this book is also for you.

Men, can I ask that you please be patient with your partner. It has become even more evident to me over the last ten or so years that men and women are extremely different... WAY more different than I thought they were though! One major difference is the way we think. I believe women are much more in touch with their emotions, are highly sensitive in vulnerable situations and can tend to over analyse things.

We also *'feel'* on an incredibly deep level, an intensity that can sometimes not be explained. 'Ineffable' is the word I recently discovered for *'not able to put into words'*.

When I started my baby making journey, I didn't have anything like this to read when I felt like I was nearly losing my mind and my only wish is that this book finds its way into as many couples or singles hands as possible and they get some comfort, or even a smile from my experience.

It has been over fifteen years in the making to get this book to the point of publication. After making some major life decisions a couple of years ago, I now have the passion and drive again to make it happen. Sometimes... in my case a lot of times, I have needed to take a good long hard look at myself in the mirror and ask, "*Is this all you are worth? Is this the best you can do?*" It is both a confronting and exhilarating feeling, and this will surely be a new chapter in my life.

There are many reasons the timing is now right to take the next step with this story. I know now I had to do a lot of learning and growing along the way before this book could have become a reality.

I also know that the things I have learnt and the people I have had the privilege of meeting, loving and being mentored by in the last ten or so years, are the only reason this is now coming to life. I have come to realise that all that had to happen first. What I always knew for sure, was this book was eventually going to happen. And the time is right now.

So, from me to you, with all my heart, I wish you much love and strength on your journey. Before I share with you my journey, let's start at the beginning.

This is the story of me, Dalya, and my husband at the time Scott, taking on the IVF roller coaster and the world with our trusty fur and feather babies, Labrador Cosmo (who we also called Cosie), our German Shepherd Vienna, and our Alexandrine Parrot George. My diary entries start from me being aged 30.

Every journey has a beginning, and this is mine...

Once Upon A Time

Ever since I can remember, I thought about and dreamed about having an amazing, loving and perfect family. Family has always been very important to me, but maybe not in the way or for the reasons you may feel it is important to you today. Let me explain.

From a young age, I dreamt about how it would be to have the perfect husband, be an awesome wife and have three or four amazing children all living in a beautiful house, with the white picket fence out the front. I believe my childhood was fairly unique and whilst I never remember wanting for anything, I look back and I recall feeling that there was always an underlying 'lack of'. At times I felt the lack of money, lack of outings, lack of holidays, and lack of cool toys. I never owned a Barbie doll or a Cabbage Patch Kid and over time I found a way to convince myself I didn't really like them anyway. I have done this with many things over the course of my life. To this day for some things, I am still not completely sure whether I *really* don't like them, or I have just convinced myself over time that I don't like them.

Over the years, I have learnt our minds and thoughts are incredibly powerful resources or weapons. It is the difference between the sharpest knife in the hands of a skilled chef or a psychopathic killer. Our thoughts can be used for ongoing good and in different circumstances can destroy lives without us even realising. That is a chapter for another day though.

The underlying 'lack of' that I felt, seemed to be something that became familiar and perhaps a little ingrained in me from a young age and continued as I got older. Now I personally think what I experienced back then was also a sense of a lack of feeling loved. Let me say here, there is a huge difference between *being* loved and *feeling* loved. I have no doubt I probably was loved, I just didn't always feel it.

My relationship with my mother was always strained, so the relationship I would have with my children was always going to be not only very special but vitally important to me. I have a few incredible memories and a few not so incredible memories that will stick with me forever. My mum passed away in 1996 at the age of fifty-two when I was twenty-six years old. Truly an amazing woman, she suffered from Multiple Sclerosis (MS) her whole life diagnosed before she was twenty-one years old and after recovering from breast cancer subsequently died of bone cancer. I also learnt that these debilitating diseases do not discriminate between young and old, male and female, kind or unkind.

Since her death, I have thought long and hard about our relationship and I have to say in the last ten years particularly, I finally understand her. I get her. I relate to her. I miss her and in some ways, I am so very like her – something I thought I'd never say.

I was born in England and in my first three or so years, was raised partly by my mother and from what I understand, mostly her husband at the time.

He raised me as his daughter and for all intents and purposes, acted as my father. A very logical decision seeing as my mother arrived back in the UK after a trip to Israel and announced she was pregnant. Unfortunately, what he did not know at the time was she was pregnant to an Israeli soldier and the baby was in fact not his.

It wasn't until she met husband number two, my stepfather and the man I'd later call Dad, that she told husband number one that I was, in fact, not his daughter. After an intense and extended custody battle and a lot of money poured into the coffers of the legal eagles, mostly on my mothers' side (funded largely by my grandmother in Canada), he eventually ran out of money and subsequently lost custody of me. By this stage Mum and her husband had a daughter and I became a big sister to Sam. In the coming months I was taken (well, smuggled) illegally out of the country and as a family we took a ferry and ended up in Ireland.

I think a part of that man, Mum's first husband, was lost the day he saw me for the last time. I contacted him some twenty years later, and we exchanged a couple of letters. I still have these letters today, telling his side of the story. I haven't read them in over fifteen years or so but still remember the underlying anger and heartbroken tone they carried. Who could blame him for feeling that way? Something he said still makes me feel emotional, which in itself may seem quite ridiculous. He said that he still carried around the photo of me in his wallet taken the last day he saw me, some twenty years later.

So, *being* loved and *feeling* love really are two completely different things.

I should say here, I never did meet my biological father and it wasn't until some years later that I was even told that my stepfather was not actually my *real* dad. I remember a friend of my mothers' coming to visit us in Ireland and I think it was around this time I was told. He said my real dad had since moved to the USA and was living there with his wife at the time.

To have the knowledge your parent doesn't want to know you, can be mind boggling to a child. For someone that tends to analyse things and has been accused of 'over thinking' things, you can imagine what was going through my head over the years as I pondered this elusive Israeli soldier.

'The Israeli', was a subject that was never spoken openly about in my extended family either. I remember some years ago, not long before my grandmother died, my sister and I were visiting her in Canada and going through some old pictures of my mum when she was young. We turned the page to see a photo of a man staring back at us. It was like I had looked into a mirror. Goose bump material! Sam and I looked at each other at the same time and then at my grandmother. I had never seen a picture of him but knew instantly who it was, and she obviously did as well. She reacted very badly and angrily removed the picture, immediately crunching it up. The incident was never spoken about again.

About eighteen months ago, through a series of unusual events, I acquired confirmation that he was alive and well living in Europe. He was practicing as a Dentist. I have seen his photograph and I have a phone number for his practice and contemplated contacting him... but never have, and probably never will. It appears he had met me a couple of times during the first few months of my life. I guess my feelings today are fairly 'vanilla' and I know that to have never known his daughter, was his loss. I also feel a sense of control as I know it is now up to me if I contact him or not.

So... after some years living in Ireland, my Mother and stepfather separated and with my sister we went back to my mother's home in Montreal, Canada. This episode lasted just two years, when whilst I was holidaying with my Aunt and Uncle, I received the phone call along the lines of; *you need to come home as we are moving to Australia next week...* I was fourteen years old.

In December 1984, my mother, Sam (then nine years old) and I, arrived on a plane into Sydney airport, with everything we owned in six suitcases and a big silver trunk. We were here to start yet our new life… again. We were picked up at the airport by Mum's second husband, Sam's Dad and we were all supposed to be playing like one big happy family.

Being a fourteen-year-old, extremely strong willed, stubborn and head strong young woman, I really wasn't happy about this move, to say the least, and I spoke to no one in my family for the next two weeks.

The next two years would continue to reinforce my feelings of 'lack of' in my life and probably mold me into some of the person I am today. Well, not probably, definitely. It would be a life exposed to alcohol, gambling, and sickness, and would ultimately end in my mother and stepfather divorcing. Through it all, I could feel that underlying 'lack of'.

For me, I just wanted to get through school, get a leaving certificate and get the hell out.

By this stage of the game, I had attended a different school about every eighteen months or so since I was about five years old and was now living in my third country. Quite a lot for a fourteen-year-old hormonal, stubborn and determined young teenager to wrap her head around.

How could I have known this would end up being a pivotal point in my life and my experiences up until then, would build character and a personality that easily made friends and survived anything that came along my way. It was the beginning of my 'can do', independent attitude and this would only strengthen over time.

In what seemed to be my mother's carefree / care *less* attitude at the time, the decision was made to move to a new house to a suburb impossible for me to commute to school from, just before my final exams in year ten. At that time, this was my school leaving certificate. I had come to the realization that university was just not going to be an option for me, at least for the time being and so my focus was purely on passing these exams and getting a job. It was the only way I saw me being able to become completely independent.

What I didn't know at the time was we were moving into a government subsidized housing commission house and this was the only one available in Sydney with wheelchair access, which my mother now needed.

My bitterness grew, and my resentful feelings smouldered away inside my teenage head, trying to comprehend 'what she was smoking' and how on earth anyone would make the decisions she was making. One thing I knew for sure is that I absolutely would not turn out to be anything like her.

I made arrangements to stay with the next-door neighbour for a couple of weeks while I completed my exams and I finished school. This in itself was a funny story. It was probably the first time and definitely not the last, that the concept of 'what you do for work is not who you are' would come up. The neighbour happened to be the bouncer of the nightclub I frequented on weekends, so he knew exactly how old I was, (way too young to be going to a nightclub and drinking alcohol), and yet my memories of him are only of kindness. He watched out for me when I was at his club and he looked after me when I stayed with him. In a strange way I believe he felt a sense of responsibility towards me, but I never asked why. He welcomed me into his home and I felt safe and that was all that mattered.

I completed my leaving certificate in 1987 and went to Secretarial College the following year. This would also be the year I moved out of home at just seventeen. I was able to find a unit to rent on my own and from here on, I became completely self-sufficient and fiercely independent. Moving out of home was not was not an easy transition but a positive one and circumstances at the time made it impossible to stay anyway. As it turned out, it became a huge milestone in my life and I was now 100% in charge of myself and what happened to me. It was probably also at this point, I learnt how to live on almost fresh air and sunshine, but despite this I was happy.

After doing some part time work, I settled into a good government job where I would remain for the next twenty-one years. This was where I later met Scott.

At sixteen I had fallen in love (as you do), and we / I planned to have our first child before I was twenty-five and the second before I was thirty years old. That relationship lasted about six years and after some interesting experiences and a whole lot of life lessons, I moved on once again.

By this stage my sister and I had grown extremely close and she was now living with me full time. My mother's health had deteriorated significantly, and she spent most of her time in the care of the next-door neighbour who looked after her and had become her trusted companion. We came to learn later that he had completely fallen in love with her. He was a very sweet and generous man and he died within a year of her. His family said it was from a broken heart.

There is a lot I have not included at this point, but I look back now, and it was no wonder having a family was so important to me. I desperately wanted someone to love unconditionally and someone who felt the same way. I wanted to provide someone with the security I never felt growing up and some consistency in life. This was becoming increasingly important to me, and despite me continually trying, I didn't feel I had experienced it so far.

I wanted to 'grow someone up', who I could teach and learn from at the same time and someone who I could make sure would never have the same childhood I'd had. What I knew for sure is that I would have lots of children and we would have wonderful experiences together.

In 1997, I decided to take a trip to Canada and travel through the Rocky Mountains to see if I could find myself and make head or tail of my life and where I was going. It was shortly before this trip that I met Scott and we would be engaged the following year and be married two years later.

About four months before we got married, we started trying to fall pregnant. It was only a short while later I started writing a diary which turned into this book.

The following diary is virtually unedited. It is almost the exact transcript written live at the time. Names have been changed and location names omitted but other than that, it is my actual journey as it happened...

Part One

The Roller Coaster Jolts Forward

Tuesday 6th February 2001

Well, today is day 21. That probably won't mean much ten years from now, but today it's significant. Well, I should say yesterday was significant. I started taking the first of two IVF related drugs. This one is a sniffing drug called Synarel. It's taken like those cold and flu nose decongestant sniffing things and for someone who thinks it's totally unnatural to stick some plastic thing up her nose and sniff at the same time, it's not a pleasant experience. I suppose the whole thing takes about two seconds and I'm sure that this is the very easy part.

So, Scott and I have been trying to have a baby since about April 1999. This is four months before we got married. I went off the pill then and we figured if worst came to worst and I fell pregnant straight away then I'd only just be showing at the wedding and the full dress would cover any little giveaways. Boy, we didn't know what we were in for. We acted like typical newlyweds on the honeymoon. By the time we got back to Sydney in October and then moved to Brisbane a week later, and still weren't pregnant we both knew something was not quite right.

I guess it all came to a head when Maria, one of our closest friends, told us she was pregnant, and I reacted pretty badly. I burst into tears and felt terrible at reacting like that to her wonderful news. I think I made her feel bad too, but this became the beginning of a beautiful friendship. Her baby boy was born on 11th August 2000, and she was just smitten with him.

So, I'd mentioned that we'd been trying to fall pregnant to a girl at work, and she suggested we see her doctor, in the city. We did this, and it turns out Scott has a low sperm count and what he does have isn't too motile. The news was devastating. We were both shattered. It took a while to come to terms with the whole situation, but we did. We started concentrating on what we could do about it.

We started with AIH, (Artificial Insemination by Husband). It required me taking a drug in tablet form called Clomid, which enabled me to produce more than the usual one egg each month. Scott had to give a sperm sample each month and this was "washed" and inseminated into me. We tried this for about four or five months in a row and then gave up. By this time, we weren't even having sex for fun anymore, and I guess this was the beginning of us losing our chemistry. We both got so focused on what we were trying to achieve that we forgot to have fun and remember just how awesome sex could be when having it for no reason.

Anyway, we upgraded our health insurance to cover IVF and it kicked in on 30th December, 2000. Just in time for the New Year. Now it's all beginning.

I'd always wanted to keep a diary of my pregnancy but didn't ever think it would be starting off like this and would all be done via a test tube. Actually, that doesn't really bother either of us. We both desperately want a baby (or two), and we'll do anything to have one. The only thing I know for sure is that a lot of time, effort and love has gone into this exercise and this baby is what we want more than anything else in the world.

Thursday 8th February 2001

They say when you play with hormones you can feel like you have more than one personality. I saw the first glimpse of Dalya 2 last night when I was completely exhausted and half asleep on the couch by 8:30pm!!! I didn't have a busy day, and I didn't get up particularly early. In fact, I didn't do much of anything, but all of a sudden, I was absolutely stuffed. I woke up this morning feeling not too bad, but by the time I got to work and went to my designated work area, at about 6am, I was in a bitch of a mood and on the verge of tears. I stopped walking for a second and thought as my eyes welled up, *"What the hell is wrong with me? It's not that bad. So, I hate work, I hate my job, and I have not made as many friends as I'd like to have, did I already mention I hate my job? I think I might hate Brisbane, but my life is really pretty good otherwise. Why the hell am I in such a vile mood?"* I snapped at the first couple of stupid customers I encountered and thought after about ten minutes *how on earth am I going to get through the day*. After a short while, I guess I got sidetracked and forgot about how shitty I'd been, so it was a pretty good day after that. I didn't feel much like socialising though, so I spent a lot of the day sitting by myself by choice. I got plenty of breaks and don't feel too bad tonight. I just looked at the clock. How can I say tonight, it's only 6pm!

Monday 12th February 2001

THE RIDE IS ABOUT TO COMMENCE!!!!!!!!!!!!!!!!

Today I got my period! How funny is that?! You must think I'm out of my mind. I haven't been this happy in ages! Probably Dalya 3 is kicking in with an extremely excited character. I suppose Dalya 2 is the shitty one; why not have Dalya 3 be the happy one? Anyway, I just had to write this down to truly show how happy I was about half an hour ago in the toilet! I got straight on the phone to the doctor's office and the ball is now rolling. I'm so excited I've got butterflies in my stomach.

Okay, take a deep breath Dalya 3 and explain properly what's happening. Okay. Well, tomorrow is Day 1, well, really Day 28 for me. I was supposed to be on Day 26 but the Synarel has a habit of making you a little later than you would usually be. I guess that confirms that I'm doing it all correctly. So, Thursday we're going into town to pick up our paraphernalia, (needles, drugs, etc.), and then the injections have to start on Sunday. This means a trip into the fertility centre early in the morning because it's better if someone professional does the first injection. Monday morning the doctor wants us both in the surgery early again. We're supposed to be on AM shift at work, so it looks like another sickie, so she can give me the next shot and actually teach Scott how to do it. They can't show me at the fertility centre on a Sunday because they're only open a few hours and there are normally heaps of women in there getting blood tests - like I used to do. So she said, "Come in on Monday and we'll do it then." Good news is he can't stuff it up either, - I checked - Nothing can go wrong.

Injections are preferably given in the morning because blood tests are taken in the morning and it's best to stay consistent. That cancels our idea of injecting at night because we're on a run of morning shifts for the next month. That just means we'll have to set the alarm for about 4am every morning even on day's off, to give me a jab. Scott will be a happy boy when I tell him he'll be getting up at 4am for the next month! Such is life I guess, it's a small price to pay. I can't believe how quickly I'm typing. I think the adrenalin is really rushing.

Okay, where was I? So then we keep taking the injections. On Day 10 I'll get a blood test (February 22) and "egg pick-up" will be somewhere between Day 14 and Day 16. There may be another trip to the doctor's office to check on the eggs etc. but I'm not sure about this. Two days later, we do the transfer and fourteen days later, I'll use Maria's pregnancy kit to tell us whether we're pregnant or not. This is so exciting I'm nearly crying. Anyway, that's the story. My God, it's finally happening!

So, I worked it out roughly, if the first day of my period is tomorrow i.e. 13 February, add seven days = 20th February, add nine months = 20 November. If I have one child, the approximate date would be 20 November!!! No, I'm not even considering that I miscarry or something else horrible happens. If I have twins it's approximately three weeks earlier, making it around 30 October. If I'm a week early, Scott gets a great birthday present 23rd October!!! It's weird because my mum's birthday is 21st October, wouldn't that be bizarre???

Bloody hell, this is really getting serious. I feel like I'm completely mad. I am *so* happy and all that's happened is my period has come. I should be in pain and cranky. Maybe there is something to fooling around with hormones.

I don't think I'll cope if something happened. I'm too wired up at the moment and it's just a bit of blood. God, when I'm pregnant look out! How do I cope if something happens? That's when I'll need Maria to turn on the phone. Actually, that's when she'll need to make up the couch!

Dalya's 1, 2 and 3!

Thursday 15th February 2001

Today we went into the doctor's office. The receptionist gave us our bag of tricks and made us sign some consent forms, so that they can get the drugs they've given us reimbursed to them.

Our little blue bag came complete with sharps container, two kinds of needles - one to draw up and another to do the injections, syringes and two strips of vials - enough for five doses of drugs. It was really bizarre. We had a chat about the drugs and she gave me a leaflet to read. The doctor also re-assured Scott that he can't do anything wrong. I can't remember what else was discussed, but we walked away excited and a bit overwhelmed. The drugs are to be kept in a cool place but not in the fridge!

She's given us enough drugs to last us until and including Thursday, when I'll get a blood test in the morning - bright and early at 7-7:30am. Then I will hang around town and call their office at midday to see if I need to have a scan. This is an internal examination that shows my follicles, and hopefully heaps of eggs. If all is well, she may say we'll do the egg collection in the following few days. It could be as early as Saturday, Sunday or Monday and that's the day Scott does his "thing" too.

She reminded us that there's always the possibility, although remote, that none of the eggs fertilise or that none of them are suitable for return. If this happens we'll have to try again next time. I don't know when exactly this would be, I'm assuming next month. If all goes well and we have suitable and mature enough eggs, they get returned two days later and then we play the waiting game. It's about fourteen days from memory, of complete frustration.

And that's the story there.

On Saturday, Dalya 4 was taking effect. I nearly threw up a couple of times on the train home from shopping on Friday. I burst into tears several times and for no apparent reason, and I walked around the house, like I was lost in an unknown world, for most of Saturday. I went to bed early and felt a lot better this morning. I nearly feel like my old Dalya 1 self now as I write this.

Saturday 17th February 2001

We arose nice and early this morning and made our way into town to the fertility centre for my first jab, complete with little blue bag in tow. Fortunately, they weren't busy, and they said it was okay for Scott to come into the room. The nurse offered to give him a crash course and we accepted willingly. We figured the more crash courses the better. Plus, it would re-assure Scott that he *could* do this without any hassles. So there we were, drugs all on the table, and Scott trying desperately to avoid cutting his fingers, and to "snap" the top of the tiny glass vial. He did manage, even with slightly trembling hands. She showed him how to draw the liquid from one vial, squirt it into the solution and then redraw it and mix it with the other vial. He then had to re-draw it all, remove the blunt needle, put on a real one, and inject. Saying it all out loud makes it sound more complicated than it actually was.

The needle itself is only about an inch long, so he can't do any damage and it can't go in far enough to go anywhere it shouldn't be going. It was then time for me to 'drop' my pants. We were told a good place to do the injection is in the top left corner of my butt cheek. Lucky for me they're big enough and Scott has plenty of room to choose from. Yes, my feeble attempt at humour.

Unfortunately, I was listening to her instructions to Scott explaining how to put the needle in etc, and they forgot to tell me that they were actually going to do it. As he put it in, I jumped and said quite loudly "*OW! that hurt!!*", and he jumped and pulled the needle right back out again. She then pointed out that this was maybe not the best thing to do for either of us, and apologised for not warning me what they were about to do.

The second time I was ready for it and didn't jump . . . as much. She told Scott to *slowly* push the syringe, so the solution also went in slowly. It actually stings if you push it in too fast. Afterwards, he copied what they do, and wiped the spot with a cotton ball to remove any drop of blood. He then swabbed the area with the little wet square. I winced and made a stupid sound and she suggested this was also not a good idea. She explained that the square has alcohol on it and it stings when you put in directly on the needle mark! This was what you did before you did the injection, and not after. Ah, you live and learn, and I think we are going to be learning a lot. She re-assured him he had done very well and said it would become easier the more he did.

So, we left feeling pretty pleased with ourselves! Scott was really proud of himself, and I was too. We both agreed that neither of us could ever be drug addicts. We couldn't deal with having to jab ourselves in the arm, or any other part of our body for that matter.

Tomorrow we get our official lesson at the doctor's office, again bright and early about 7:30am. We're then heading over to the Casino where we will meet Dad for brekkie. I think he's coming around to the idea of being a grandfather and made a comment about "*there go my weekends.*" Neither of us said anything, but I will remind him at a later and more appropriate time of his comment.

Oh, I'm supposed to keep taking the Synarel until specifically told to stop. God only knows who will emerge this week taking the Synarel and injections. If we are really unlucky we might even get up to Dalya 20! So, I only stop the Synarel when she wants me to ovulate... I think.

Dalya 1, 2, 3, and the latest addition to our happy household Dalya 4!!

Friday 2nd March 2001

Well, I'm writing this a bit behind and there's a lot to catch up on.

A week ago, Monday (18th Feb) 2001

As planned, we went into the surgery for our crash course. It was much the same stuff as the fertility centre, except Scott got a couple of extra tips including an easier way to break the top off the vials. It was also suggested that the upper thigh is a better injecting site. We were to continue the injections every morning around about the same time. We decided on 4am because we were on a run of morning shifts for the next 2 weeks or so. We then had to go for a blood test on day 10 which is Thursday.

It all sounded straight forward but we quickly discovered it was easier said than done. Some of the mornings weren't too bad, others were disastrous. I was starting to get really shitty every time Scott went near me with the needle. It wasn't his fault and I know he was trying to do the right thing and didn't want to hurt me. Most of the time, it didn't really hurt, and I just got anxious and a little sweaty and stressed just before the injection. If you get it in a vein, well it's not really a vein I don't think, maybe a blood vessel; it leaves a dot of blood. It can really hurt when the needle goes in or the fluid itself and because you only have surface veins to go by, they are not always that clear.

So, **Thursday 21st February 2001,** I went into town. I had a blood test and then went for a scan. My oestrogen was way up, and the scan looked good. The doctor was very happy. She asked how my tummy had been and I said *a bit bloated every few days but nothing major.* She said this was normal and would probably get worse over the next few days. She gave us five more days of injections and said to take the last one on Wednesday morning with my last Synarel sniff. There was then a single special injection to release the eggs on Wednesday night. Finally, the injections would all be over! Woo Hoo!

Today is Friday 2nd March 2001

This morning was the beginning of the end of this little part of the adventure. This morning was egg collection. We had to be at the fertility centre at 6:45am to book in and I went into theatre at 7:30am. They continued the paperwork and then Scott and I split up and I got changed into a cotton gown, with little paper slippers and paper undies and hat. I had to remove all my jewellery and I had to shower with a "surgisponge" in the morning and not use soap. The surgisponge is like this spongy square that lathers up in the shower, so you do actually feel like you're washing yourself. I had showered and washed my hair before I went to bed last night anyway as I was not sure what to expect.

So, there I was sitting in the waiting room in my hospital gown and a terry towelling robe, waiting to be called to see the anaesthetist. I started talking to an Indian girl and she said it was her 6th try! I felt really bad for her, poor thing. She said her mother in law is a bitch and driving her and her husband crazy. She was so sick of her getting involved in their business! I was still stuck on six tries! Imagine six tries! Scott and I are stressed out enough as it is; I don't think we'd even go for two let alone six more tries. I guess we'll cross that bridge when we come to it.

So, I was called into another room and saw the anaesthetist. He seemed really nice. I was then led into a larger room, very similar to theatre rooms on the show ER or those other hospital tv shows. There were about five nurses all dressed the same with hospital gowns on and complete with their own paper shoes and hats. My doctor was also there, and she would be performing the procedure.

I lay on the bed and they asked me a couple of questions about work and the next thing I knew I woke up in a ward feeling very groggy. It was about 9am. Scott was there with me and it took me the next hour or so to completely come out of the anaesthetic. I had a sandwich and cup of tea and Scott had given his sample about 8:40am.

Scott's observations of '*the room*' were very bizarre. He said he was handed a key and he went down a corridor where there was a locked door. There were porno videos and magazines and heaps of tissues and specimen jars as well as a bed. He said it was really weird, but he did what he had to do, albeit sheepishly.

It turns out, they harvested ten eggs and apparently this was good. They are hoping that at least five fertilise. On Monday at 8am, all being well, they'll put two embryos back. The plan is that they make their journey to the lining and hopefully implant themselves ready to start growing.

We then waited for the scientists to give us the go ahead, and we were on our way about 10:15am.

So now it's just a matter of waiting and seeing what happens over the weekend. They are going to ring me in the morning anyway and see if I'm okay. They will also tell me how many eggs fertilised and to confirm Monday's 8am appointment.

The only side effect I guess I know I have is severe bloating. It's like having really bad period pain without the period. This is partially due to fluid retention I think and should go away in the next few days. So, we were home just after lunch and I had a sleep this afternoon, which I think I really needed. I'm not working tomorrow, as they said I should give myself another day to recover from the anaesthetic properly. That's the way it is at the end of Friday 2nd March.

Saturday 3rd March 2001

Well, I had the day off work today, and I got a call from the nurse at the fertility centre around 8am this morning as expected. They do a routine call to all patients the next morning to see if they slept okay, and to make sure they are not having any bad reactions or a quick onset of hyper stimulation. I wasn't feeling too bad after a good sleep, but she was quick to say that the bloating would probably get worse throughout the day. This was very true. Anyway, as agreed she'd rang the lab before she called me and guess what? WE HAVE SEVEN!!!!!!!!! FERTILISED EGGS!!!!!!!!!! I know our doctor was hoping for around five, so seven is amazing. The nurse even seemed excited. My God, seven! This means that we would still only put the best two back but reinforces the possibility that we're probably going to have twins! It also means that the others can be frozen, so I won't need to take all the drugs again next time. And, if it didn't work this time, I could just get a straight embryo transfer next time, the same as what we're having on Monday.

So, this morning I dug out my "*What to expect when you're expecting*" book by Heidi Murkoff. It is full of fascinating and interesting information and some pretty incredible details, I was enthralled.

Scott rang around lunchtime. He had rung just after 8am and was thrilled to hear about our little eggs. So, how am I feeling? SORE!! I've ached *all* day and spent most of the time holding my stomach and trying to drink as much fluid as possible. I even resorted to paracetamol. Apparently, this is normal and quite safe to take a mild pain killer.

Dalya,
Queen of Bloating Tummies!

Monday 5th March 2001

This morning, we were in the fertility centre theatres again at 7:30am. We were both tense, but excited at the same time. We spoke to the doctor before the transfer and she said there was one really good embryo that had already divided into eight cells and was a real goer. This would be the one she'd put back, if we were happier with just transferring one, then that was what we should do. So, we donned paper slippers, hats and gowns and once again returned to theatre. I was once again lucky enough – not, to have my legs in stirrups and Scott was beside me this time, a bit spun out, I think. The doctor 'got me ready' and then the scientist came in with the embryo in a fine tube thing. It was very similar to the AIH and didn't hurt. It took only a few seconds and it was all over. This was going to be it now; it was totally out of our hands. It was time to let nature take its course. I was given pessaries to insert for the next sixteen days and then could take a pregnancy test and see if I was in fact pregnant.

Wednesday 7th March 2001

Pessaries, very glamorous things they are. Like a huge Omega 3 tablet that breaks down in your body and leaves a white creamy residue.

"*Just insert them like a tampon*", they say. "*thanks, but no thanks*", I reply. Anyway, I'm being good, and I am doing just that, every night for the next fourteen nights. I'm starting to picture what me with no dignity looks like and I think Scott is in for a shock.

I'm really looking forward to being pregnant and really, really hope this works. In the end we only ended up putting one embryo back because the thought of twins scared us a little too much first go. The doctor was so great with it all. Before we went into the theatre room she came into the waiting room and chatted with us to see if we were both okay. She also wanted to confirm how many we'd decided to put back. When we voiced our concerns, she said it was perfectly understandable and even hinted that we were among the majority of couples that go through this.

She said we can always put two back later and if

we're at all concerned then stick with one - the best one of course. She said that it was normal for us to be totally stressed out and this was a common feeling. The flip side of this was some people didn't think enough about what happens in nine months' time. They are so excited about putting two back and then two babies are born and they're a bit bewildered. She reassured us that we were definitely doing the right thing and said we had other chances anyway. If worst came to worst and this one didn't work, or even if it did, the embryo's stay frozen until we need them next time.

I'm so glad we got onto her, she's such a wonderfully caring doctor and we both feel really comfortable with her. I think it is going to make all the difference! So, we left with her saying good luck. She'd have her fingers crossed and to call the surgery in sixteen days one way or the other and we'd take it from there. HOW EXCITING!!!!!!!!!!!

Thursday 15th March 2001

Em1 is my little name for embryo 1 and all is well so far. I don't want to pre-empt anything by getting too excited, but I should point out a few things early in the piece. Today is day 13 and counting, plus it's nearly over and this week has flown by, so I'm thinking the wait won't be that bad after all. The last few days will be the hardest and I can see us cracking and doing a pregnancy test early. I don't know if it will give a correct reading, but I think that pregnancy tests generally only give a false negative and not a false positive. Anyway, we'll see.

Point two; I wee'd last night before I went to bed, about 9pm. I was up twice in the night and again when I woke up this morning at 3:30am. That is four times in a six-hour period. I wee'd about four times during the day at work as well, and I've wee'd twice since I've been home, about three and a half hours. I haven't drunk an excessive amount of liquid and while I'm on the subject, for the first time in my life ... how do I say this ... I was actually constipated!!! I have never ever before been constipated and today was most uncomfortable. I sat there for ages and ... well anyway, moving right along...

So, I'm hoping without hoping too much that these little indicators are all positive signs. I guess I'll know if I keep weeing tonight and tomorrow and for the next few weeks. I'm thinking that I shouldn't be getting symptoms yet though, the embryo should have only burrowed this week -

fingers crossed eh.

Friday 16th March 2001

Scott and I decided early on in the week that today we would go up the coast to what was supposed to be a big shopping centre and have a good day together, just the two of us and leave all our stresses behind at home. This was a great idea and it was a good day.

Unfortunately, I have a secret and I suspect that I'm not actually pregnant after all. I got some little spotting early this morning and rang the doctor. Scott doesn't know any of this because I don't want to upset him before it's confirmed. I know that when the embryo imbeds itself, there is often some spotting and some spotting *is* normal in early pregnant people. I haven't had much more than that today, but it's exactly the same as the beginning of a period for me. I'm so numb after everything that's happened; I just don't know if I can even cry any more. I've come so close to telling him today and so close to bursting into tears I keep thinking what if it's just that and nothing more? What if it's just spotting? I may actually be pregnant. All my gut feelings say I'm not though and I'll just have to wait and see what happens in the next twenty-four hours. I should know by then. I'm assuming that if it is a period, that it will come in tonight or tomorrow and put me out of my misery or should I say, bury me under it.

Do I dare go near the bathroom again? I just want to know. The waiting is killing me. God, I just want to know one way or the other. It's making me nuts. The last two weeks have been unbelievably stressful for both Scott and I and at times I've seriously felt like I'm losing my mind.

Wednesday 21st March 2001

I'M DEFINITELY PREGNANT!!!!!!!!!!

I just got off the phone with the doctor's surgery and guess what? As of Sunday, I'm five weeks pregnant!!!!!

AAAAAAAAAAAAAAAhhhhhhhhhhhhhhh!!!!!!!! How bizarre! She told me how they count it, but I can't remember now. It's something to do with the date of transfer. My God, it's sinking in now, it's really real. I'm really pregnant. Nearly five weeks pregnant! Anyway, she also said my levels are excellent. They want a level above 500, I think of HCG, and mine is 778. I guess that's good. She said, we still have to be very careful, but we can get excited we're definitely pregnant and it all looks good. She's going to send me out a pamphlet on stuff not to eat and other things to avoid. Can't wait for that one! I bet they don't say anything about underwire bras! Hee Hee I just had to throw that one in. Maria has been harping on about how I can't wear underwire bras anymore and definitely not when bub is born. Apparently maternity bras don't come with underwire anyway! Who knew?

The other big news is that my first ultrasound is scheduled for 11th April during my seventh week and I will be going through this doctor for everything. Oh, estimated time of arrival for Em1 is 25th November!

Dalya and Em1 (and a stunned husband)

Saturday 24th March 2001

I've been keeping up my fluids and I've been going wee, wee, wee all the way home, all day and all night. This is good fun! Other than that, I feel fine, great, and terrific and am hoping with all hope that everything continues to go well.

Tomorrow is a milestone for me, five weeks, and I'm hoping I'll start to feel pregnant, so far, I feel totally normal. My boobs have been pretty tender the last few days and were even sore on Wednesday. I suppose this is also pretty normal. I hope it doesn't mean they're growing already! So, I am now waiting to receive the pamphlet on stuff that I shouldn't be eating, or at least staying away from, and I'm looking forward to reading it. The only thing I know at the moment is shellfish! Luckily, I hardly eat it, although I did feel like Chinese prawns on Wednesday. Does it count if they're cooked and Chinese style? I suppose so.

My sister Sam is *sooo* excited. I spoke to her about five times on Wednesday and her best friend rang me as well. She kept saying "*Oh my God, I'm having a baby, this is sooo exciting!*" She's so funny. She said, *finally mum is going to have a grandchild*. I told her, it served Mum right for having to wait this long; she hasn't exactly helped me out here.

P.S. Em almost sounds like a girl hey? Scott decided he doesn't really want to know what bub is. I do though, so it will probably be a surprise for him. Also, he said he doesn't want anyone else to know what sex it is or what names we choose. He's pretty pleased with himself I must say!

Wednesday 28th March 2001

We're having dinner with Dad tomorrow night, so no doubt the question of how the IVF went will be raised and I'd say we'll end up telling him. It's just easier that way than lying and then hearing all the words of encouragement given.

So, I was flicking through my "*What to expect . . .*" book and was very pleased to hear that everything I am feeling at the moment is totally normal. Emotionally, I appear to be normal. Sad, happy, cranky, scared, excited and sometimes if I'm really lucky, I feel them all at the same time! Also, the irritating stitchy type pains I've had the past day or two, on and off, across my belly, are also normal. It's not a pain, as in I have pains in my tummy, but more a niggling,' *I know it's there little pain'* and it is not constant. Apparently, this is my uterus stretching! You've gotta love that! As Scott said, this has to be a good sign; it means something is growing in there! Also, my boobs haven't been as tender the last few days, but I take my bra off and they just seem . . . well I can't describe it as anything other than heavy. I noticed that I had a slight line across them last night too, from the elastic in the lace and was horrified to think they were growing already. I'm not even six weeks yet! Anyway, according to the book this is also normal, and I can expect to see lovely blue veins appearing as well. For the record, it would not be unusual for my breasts to start growing now, but they describe it as 'swelling' and 'fullness'. This would describe me exactly!

I'm still feeling really tired at times too, although I haven't managed to pin point whether this is my newest growth or the shift work. I'm not convinced of this *symptom*. However, the books say that if I haven't been eating properly then this can also contribute to me being tired.

Apparently the little one is starting to suck me dry and making my body work overtime, building a spine and other bits and pieces. I really have to start eating properly. I didn't get up in time for brekkie today but have had a salad roll and have spaghetti with cottage cheese for dinner. I was too lazy and couldn't think to work out anything other than that. Scott made a beef stir-fry and the smell of the meat was pretty yuck. This seems to be an on and off thing. I had vegetarian noodles last night with chilli and was *so* full afterwards I wished I hadn't eaten it all. Having said that, my tummy wasn't too happy this morning and probably why I didn't have anything more than a salad roll for lunch.

My sense of smell is something I'm much more aware of too. It has become quite acute! I know this is a classic symptom of pregnancy but still wonder if it's my imagination and that I would have normally been aware of certain smells anyway. For example, I could smell the hokkien noodles in the boiling water which I don't think I've ever noticed. The smell of the meat cooking seemed really strong too. I could even smell the oil he'd put in the pan. Pretty weird hey?

Okay, so I guess I'm pregnant right? I still don't feel any real difference though, although I guess everything I've described above *is* different to how I would normally feel.

Thursday 5th April 2001

Well, I've been feeling pretty yucky - nauseous yucky, not so much to the point of wanting to throw up, but pretty sickly and squirgly in the tummy. I wasn't too bad this morning though, which of course worried me because I hadn't had the stitch pain thing either, and just felt tired.

Then later in the day, my stitchy thing came back and all was well with the world. I seem to have started eating more frequent but smaller meals too. I can't eat as much in one sitting as I used to. A smorgasbord would be wasted on me these days. I tend to eat something littlish about every four to five hours. I've been having a cup of tea before I leave the house in the morning over the last few days and this seems to settle me until I get to work. Then I have a piece of toast before starting. Three hours later by the breakfast break, I'm really hungry again. The nausea only seems to be very early in the morning at the moment. I suppose it could still be my body rebelling over the early morning starts. This shift has been particularly painful!

I just found out my neighbour was eleven weeks pregnant and she lost the baby! I know I shouldn't be thinking about it, but bloody hell! ... NO, I won't even think about it. I definitely won't write it. I can't imagine how she must feel.

Wednesday 11th April 2001

The next few weeks will be busy and it's exactly how I wanted it, although I'm a little worried I'll sleep through it all. I'm going to sleep between 7-8pm every night and sleeping till 6-7am the next morning. That's like ten and a half hours sleep every night. I go back to work tomorrow for three AM shifts and one late PM shift. I'm dreading it and start to panic that I won't cope with the late one every time I think of it. I cannot believe how stuffed I am by just 7pm though. It's totally crazy. I am glad to hear this will only last another seven or so weeks . . . aaaaaahhhhhh! I can't even complain or tell people why I feel like crap and I can't concentrate. I just want a little corner to have a nap in!

With any luck the first time I tell our friends from Sydney, will be when they see me in a few weeks and I'm really hoping that this baby is growing outward by then so I will have something to show. We're hoping not to tell anyone till about thirteen or fourteen weeks.

I've thought a lot about losing babies recently and I guess it's something you worry about from the time you find out you're pregnant till birth day; what with all the things that can go wrong from one stage to another. I was thinking about Sudden Infant Death Syndrome (SIDS) the other day actually and thinking that when the baby's born, I should be finally at the point that I can stop worrying about them but will more than likely be one of those pathetic parents that check on them four million times a night. I was like that with the puppies too. I guess you just get used to it.

Sunday 15th April 2001

My next ultrasound is on Wednesday 9th May. By then I'll be just over eleven weeks. Around that time, I need to start thinking about two tests I can have done for Down Syndrome (DS).

a) a neck thickness which is done by a scan at twelve weeks or

b) a blood test at sixteen weeks.

These tests only detect 60-70% of DS though and if the number comes back greater than whatever is not the good number, then you go to the amniocentesis at sixteen weeks. In this case there is a higher chance of miscarriage.

The eighteen-week scan is the big one and will detect 25% of DS and two thirds of all other abnormalities in the baby. The doctor didn't seem too concerned whether I had DS testing or not, but she said she would not suggest I go to the amnio at this point. So far, we have the perfect pregnancy and didn't want to risk anything including miscarriage at this stage. She said in her first pregnancy she got tested and in the second she didn't get anything done. Like she said, it's only 60-70% of cases, so even with all the testing in the world; it still may not pick anything up anyway. But at the end of the day, she said it was our choice. I'll probably just get a blood test done. This sounds simple and easy and no risk involved.

She also said my age was of no concern, so the chances of DS would be much less than say if I was 37 or older. So, I'm not really sure why I'm even bothering. I'll see what happens, I may just not bother. I asked her what her opinion would be, and she said it was entirely up to us. As she hasn't pushed toward testing, I'm inclined not to bother. The eighteen-week scan is supposed to be the biggy and if anything is not okay, I'm assuming it would probably be picked up then.

Scott has changed his mind once or twice about knowing whether Em is a boy or girl. He said it would be more practical to know and I asked why? We're going to go with Maria's idea of staying pretty neutral as far as clothing and decorating so it won't matter what Em is.

I was flicking through my book, "*Up the Duff*" by Kaz Cooke, today and there's one bit in it (page 83 to be exact) where she said "*Nausea stops suddenly for a whole day. Oh my God. Nausea starts again. Thank God. Bloody Nausea.*" I just need to say here this is me! Well at least it was for a day last week. I'm a bit like her I'm afraid, when she says she's nauseous all the time. When I think of it, I cannot honestly say I ever really feel 100% great. Yeah right, morning sickness my ass! They should just call it constant yuckiness. And I get to have this for the next few weeks. That's so great!!!!!!! Not. Page 85 explained what's going on with my poo's too. That was really helpful! I really should start reading this book properly again, it's great.

Not too much difference in my boobs yet, they're tender and they're big. I haven't noticed any veins as such and no darkening of the areola they say can happen.

I bought a jar of decaf coffee just after I found out I was pregnant and have only had one spoon of it. I'm a regular coffee drinker but haven't felt the urge. I am drinking one or two cups of tea a day though. It seems lighter on my sick tummy I think. Other than that, I haven't really gone off anything as such. The smell of the cigarettes is getting to breaking point though and I've snapped at Scott a few times. He's not smoking anywhere near me, but the smell seems to have intensified about 1 million percent and that's all I smell when I'm near him.

It's really off putting, and he knows it makes me sick. It's like the nausea, it just seems constant.

8 weeks today.

Wednesday 18th April 2001

My life has become a circle of sleep, eat, go to work, come home, sleep, eat, go to work come home since Sunday morning. I'm up at least three times during the night and this does not include the before I go to sleep wee and the wake up wee. My God, how much water do I have in me???

I got a call from the doctor's office yesterday and guess what? Actually, I was initially worried when I got the message but figured it can't be something bad because they wouldn't have anything to tell me, I'm not waiting on anything. Anyway, they wanted me to book into the Hospital for November! There were only about three or four spots left and she said I have to book today to ensure a spot and the doctor we have been seeing doesn't deliver anywhere else. How exciting eh? It's all happening. I rang the hospital and they are going to send me out some paperwork and a list of courses. Oh my gosh, I can't wait to receive that.

Nauseated, sleepy and ready to retire!

Friday 20th April 2001

My nausea eased off almost totally yesterday although it did return. It was not as bad but enough to know I think I'm still pregnant this afternoon. Plus, I didn't get up a million times during the night. I think I only got up twice actually. Now all I have to hope for is I have a horrible sleep and that I am up again tonight. I rang the doctor this morning and her receptionist said not to panic just yet and if I'm still worried next week I can always go in for a scan. She also said that if something has gone wrong it can take up to two weeks for the blood to come in. Great! This is horrible. I rang Maria panicked at 8:20am, She must think I'm a nutcase. I'm off to consult my pregnancy books to see if I can find anything in them about what's going on.

Saturday 21st April 2001 - 6:40am

I was going to write earlier but thought I might just fall asleep again. Actually, I didn't sleep too well at all. I woke up really early and sort of dozed and just lay there worrying about what I seem to be convincing myself of and wondering what the hell I am going to do now. I just don't feel anything anymore. Even my boobs aren't sore, I don't feel sick and I'm not weeing as much. I'm not convinced its hormones and have gotten to the stage of panic that at 8:30am I'm going to ring the doctor and see what she says. I'm hoping she'll let me come in this weekend sometime and just check for a heartbeat. That's all I want to know. I'll pay extra if that's what it takes. I doubt she'll let me come in and she's probably not even the doctor on call, but this is driving me nuts. It's way worse than waiting to see if I'm even pregnant or not. And if the blood takes up to two weeks to start, I'll be a complete basket case by then.

I just have to know if everything is okay and if it isn't well, I've suspected as much the last forty-eight hours anyway. So, I'm sitting here in the study, a mess and thinking how glad I am that no one can see me at the moment. I'm happy to be proven wrong about this and to hear the words, "*it is just hormones and look at the screen, there's the heartbeat going strong*", but in all honesty; I don't think that's what is going to happen. I guess I have to work out how to tell her all this on the phone without sounding like a mental patient crying and blubbering all over the place.

God this is up there with the hardest things I've ever had to deal with and the stupid thing is I'm not even sure about the baby one way or the other. I think my gut instinct tells me something is different and I'm just praying and hoping it is just hormones. I've got all the hospital papers on the printer here and am wondering if I'll end up filling them in after all. I know this is not hormones. Who am I kidding? God, I hope I'm wrong about this.

Maria has already finished the embroidery on a towel for Em. And this is making me really sad because if something has gone wrong...

Later

I just spoke to the other doctor that works in my doctor's office, (they take it in turns to be on call on weekends) and she said to show up at the surgery on Monday morning and see my usual doctor directly. She reckons it's better that way because if something has gone wrong she can fix it all up for me in the one go. I tried to suggest that I could maybe come in this weekend, but she said it would be better to sit tight until Monday. I asked her if any of this was normal and she said that they do see it every now and then, and it could also be a result of the IVF drugs. I'm just not convinced!

Sunday 22nd April 2001

Just a very quick entry to say I think the panic is over. After spending most of yesterday morning in tears and then going over to one of my girlfriend's to ask her how she knew she was having a miscarriage, I think she had two or maybe three, my sickness and tender boobs came back with a vengeance late this afternoon. I felt as sick as I have when I got up this morning and I think I nearly gave myself a nervous breakdown for nothing.

So, the plan at the moment is I'm not going to go into the surgery as planned at 8:00am tomorrow, but I will ring early and tell them what happened and if they think it's warranted, I'll make an appointment for during the week sometime.

Anyway, I'm happy to report I'm feeling as blah as

ever! God, imagine being a person who was not happy unless they were feeling yucky. What a weirdo eh? Who the hell has Scott married?

Pregnant again.

Saturday 28th April 2001

As far as Em is going, well, everything seems to be great. My nausea has now gone much to my pleasure, this pretty much went after about Monday or Tuesday this week, and my boobs are only just tender. I'm still getting up anywhere up to four times during the night which is a little annoying, but that's fine.

I bought the book *Conception Pregnancy and Birth* by Dr Miriam Stoppard yesterday. Scott was fascinated with it and couldn't believe some of the pictures. I took it back to bed with me this morning and skimmed through the first few chapters. God I can't wait! I'm really excited. Oh, I think I'm eating heaps too. I seem to have put on weight. According to the book I shouldn't put on more than about 2kgs during the first trimester. I think I've topped that already, but I daren't go near scales. I'll be happy when I stop looking fat in the mirror and look more round. I am still eating less meat than before but pretty much anything else that comes across my path. Sam made an awesome lasagne last night and we had it with salad and I was SO full afterwards. Well, I'm off to make a cup of tea now; I am still off the coffee despite the new jar of decaf in the cupboard.

P.S. Week 10 tomorrow!

Thursday 3rd May 2001

I had a huge sleep last night. I dozed off on the couch about 7:30pm and then went to bed about 8:30pm. I woke up four times during the night and once to throw the dogs out and then didn't budge until 8:30am this morning. It was great. At one point I woke up on my belly too, so I don't know if that's a good thing or not. I haven't been able to sleep on my tummy since about the sixth week. I seem to remember Maria saying though that her boobs were fine again around this time. I'll just be happy after this ultrasound on Wednesday when I know for sure everything is still all in the right places and all is okay.

Wednesday 9th May 2001

Miscarriage confirmed.

Thursday 10th May 2001

I'm writing this at 7:00am on Thursday 10th May, because if I tried to explain how I'm feeling in days or weeks from now, I don't think I could.

Saturday, I started spotting and went to my faithful books. It said to contact the doctor straight away but that it was not necessarily a bad thing. I figured I had my 11½ week ultrasound booked for yesterday morning anyway, so I'd just wait until then and see what happened. I did panic though but managed to hold it together until I got to the doctor's surgery. Scott was still in Melbourne and I didn't tell him what was going on with me as there was not much he could do if anything was wrong anyway. Plus, if everything was fine, I didn't want him on the next flight home for no reason.

I had my first external ultrasound which was kind of special, but my nerves were getting the better of me and my hands were shaking and my heart pounding. As I lay on the table I could hear myself breathing heavily and I was terrified. The doctor confirmed my worst fears at that point and decided to do a vaginal scan. Again, she confirmed, there was no heartbeat and only a sac left.

So, at this point what are you supposed to feel? I do not blame myself or anyone else and logic tells me that it's because of an abnormality and everything happens for a reason. There is no way to tell when the embryo self-aborted but it never developed to the point it should have at 11½ weeks. I was looking forward to seeing a little head and miniature body and little webbed feet and hands. I saw nothing, not even the visible blob we saw at 7½ weeks. I was shattered and dumbfounded and stunned and so intensely disappointed and just plain devastated.

After the scan I just sat for a while and while I cried, the doctor talked. She assured me there was no reason why we couldn't start again almost immediately, and next time round, I'll go in for weekly scans, so she can monitor what's going on. This will mean we will both have peace of mind. She said after the curette, within about two weeks I should get a period and then the following period we can begin again.

I left the office crying my eyes out and headed for the car, where I had to break the news to Scott in Melbourne on the mobile. He was shattered as well and said he was heading to the airport and would catch the next available flight home to me. I headed for my Dad's house.

I spent most of this day bursting into tears whenever I thought about it. And the pain I have felt in my heart since that disastrous 'nothing' on the screen is suffocating. I am feeling completely deflated and am so glad that Scott is back in Brisbane and here with me now. I know we will get through this together.

So next step was I needed to have a curette done, a medical term for a clean out, which is being done this morning. It is performed under general anaesthetic and at the fertility centre. Shortly after that, I should get a period and at the beginning of my next period, we'll start monitoring for the best day and start again with an embryo transfer.

It's amazing to think that I've been thinking the last few weeks that I'm pregnant but haven't been at all. The closest we can pin point it down to is a few weeks ago when I lost all my pregnancy symptoms, that was around 9½ weeks. Scott and I both think something happened that weekend. Maybe it tried to correct itself if that's even possible? Maybe that was why I was sick again on the Sunday or maybe it was all in my head. I know as of that week the symptoms tapered off and since then I've been feeling fine. It's no wonder! There wasn't anything wrong with me or right for that matter.

So now we're just trying to get used to all the plans that

won't be happening. There will be no Em for Christmas and no telling our friends when we go away in a few weeks. There will be no starting to buy nursery stuff and all the rest of the things I'm sure people think about after a miscarriage.

So, I'm sitting here at 7:10am and am off to the fertility centre for about 9:45am. The procedure takes place at 11am and I'll be so glad when it's all over. I just want today to be over so we can start to try and get some sort of normality back in our lives. That sounds so stupid doesn't it? Ha! Normality! What exactly is that when you play this game? I guess I'm wishing away the next two months, so we can start this madness again.

We'll find out today what the story is with frozen embryos and I just pray that we don't have to go through all the drug business again. If we do though, we've decided we'll just grin and bear it and we will try and try and try until we get us this baby. It's a bit of a change in mindset since a few weeks ago eh? I think I was feeling so sick and tired of everything and that we'd be lucky to go for two tries let alone any more. I guess that was what I was thinking at the time but now I think we've got the bug and will continue to try until it happens, and it WILL happen.

Friday 11th May 2001

Yesterday was one of the most horrible days ever. Actually, yesterday and Wednesday were both horrible. We got into the fertility centre about 9:45am on Wednesday and both burst into tears at the counter before we'd even said, "*hi, we're Dalya and Scott and we're here for* ..." The nurses were great as usual and moved us into an office where I tried my best to pull myself together which was successful for a couple of minutes. Scott was amazing and even though tears filled his eyes, he filled out all the paperwork as I sat there bawling. I cried on and off for the next little while and then it was time to part ways and for me to once again don my paper shoes and cotton gown, but this time not for an egg collection.

I sat in the waiting room and didn't even look at the other two girls that were there casually flicking through the magazines. I thought '*they're obviously not here for a curette. I wish I wasn't either*'. I tried to watch TV, but my mind kept wandering back to the reason why I was here, and my eyes kept filling with tears. The anaesthetist came and called me just before 11.30am and by the time I'd walked the ten or fifteen meters to her office I was crying all over the place again. It was just so hard to get it together. I did my best to answer the questions and she was very patient. I put on my paper hat and went into the familiar theatre room where I'd been just a few weeks earlier for the egg collection. My doctor was there and I cried again when I saw her. She asked how Scott was and I said 'shattered'. I just wanted it all to be a bad dream, but it wasn't. The tears pour down my cheeks now as I think about this and it's only the second time I've cried today. Not bad considering it's 1:11pm already.

Anyway, I drifted off to sleep and awoke in the recovery area with Scott holding my hand. I'll never forget the look on his face. His bottom lip was trembling and his eyes red from crying as he smiled feebly and asked how I was feeling. Once again, a big tear rolled down my cheek.

I had something to eat and when I'd come out of the anaesthetic properly, we went home. I retired to the bedroom pretty much straight away and stayed there for the rest of the day and night. My heart was breaking and my stomach was killing me with cramps. I had taken a couple of paracetemols at the hospital and took some more later in the night. Scott kept coming up to check on me and bring me fresh water and give me a hug. He'd kept in touch with Sam and Dad so they both knew what was happening. I rang Maria when I got home. She's been so amazing through all this I don't know what I'd have done without her. She seemed pretty happy to hear from me and glad that I'd rang to say we were alive and well. One of my girlfriends came over later with a Chrysanthemum plant, which I didn't see until I came downstairs after she'd left, and this again reduced me to tears.

This is probably a good time to put in parts of the letter that Scott wrote to family in Canada. It sort of describes how he's feeling at the moment, or was last night…

"Thanks for writing. Yeah, it has been a while since we last heard from each other, and I suppose there's probably a bit of catching up to do. First of all, I suppose a rather sad note. In February we started the IVF (in vitro fertilisation) programme after it became apparent that my boys would never be up to the job. This was a major bummer, but we figured if this was the only way, well so be it. So, we jumped

on board the IVF roller coaster. It was a lot harder on Dalya than myself, though I have to say the whole process was wearing thin on me after a while.

The lead up involved us having to get up at 4:00am every day for sixteen days, it seemed like sixteen bloody months, so I could inject Dalya with a cocktail of hormones to stimulate her ovaries. You can imagine that this is not the most thrilling thing in the world to do, considering my initial attempts at injections were akin to watching an episode of Mr Bean. You can imagine with hormones running rampant in Dalya's body the impact it had on her. It was a pretty tough time on both of us, but we survived, and I think the both of us became stronger for it. We had to do an egg collection which meant that Dalya had to go under a general anaesthetic, I then did my little thing, in a private room of the building equipped with dirty videos and magazines, and as a result the doctors fertilised some of the eggs they harvested. We were lucky, they got five embryos, and we put one back into Dalya, and then waited for nature to do its work.

So, we waited a couple of weeks, rather impatiently I must say, until the day before the designated day, when we jumped the gun and did a pregnancy test. To our delight, it came up positive, so Dalya trotted off to the Doctor the next day or so to get it confirmed. This was around the 25th of March. So, another four weeks went by, and Dalya was seven weeks pregnant. With the symptoms, nausea, food aversion, weeing all the time etc. everything was on course, though at that early stage, everything's a lottery. Off we went for an ultrasound, and it was the most amazing thing, a little shapeless blob, with a tiny little heart pounding sixteen to the *dozen. I was amazed. The doc said that she was very happy, everything was where it should be, and that we would be back in another four weeks for our eleven-week scan.*

Around week nine, Dalya had a fright, because the symptoms disappeared for a weekend, a couple of phone calls were made, which resulted in her getting an appointment for a scan on the Monday morning. Sunday night the symptoms reappeared, and I've never seen anyone so delighted to be sick all the time again. So, we dropped the scan idea. I was in Melbourne for three days, doing family tree research and just doing the touristy thing bit. Anyway, yesterday was my last day down there, and Dalya had previously organised her scan on that day (unfortunately poor planning on both our parts meant that I was in Melbourne, but that the important scan was the eighteen weeks one). I was sitting in the State Library of Victoria huddled over a computer, when the phone rang. I knew it would be Dalya, and was worried that she hadn't rung by now, and she started off by asking me to sit down. The news was not good. Sometime between week seven and week eleven the embryo had failed to kick on, and subsequently all there was left was the amniotic sac.

I couldn't believe it. I wasn't due home till later that night but managed to drop everything. I ran back to the hotel, caught two trams, a bus and a plane back to Brisbane, so I could get to Dalya. Fortunately, I was able to get her Dad to spend time with her before I made my appearance, he was wonderful. The flight was a long one (well, it seemed long although it was only really two hours). So, I got home, and Dalya was waiting at the plane for me, it was obviously an emotional homecoming.

Today was the rather unpleasant business of a curette, to put it quite bluntly, to clean Dalya out, and start again. There was another general anaesthetic involved. This time it was a very quick process, the recovery time was longer, and we were back home by 4:00pm. As a result, she has a really sore tummy, and is obviously very emotional. My heart is breaking to see her suffering like she is now, but I know we will get through it. The neighbours have been wonderful; one of my closest friends Maria is always in touch. Dalya's on the phone now to another one of her girlfriends. We were saving writing until we got the "official" all clear, and to give you the wonderful news, but instead you get this long-winded piece of self-pity. Well at least it's good therapy for me. Dalya will be off work for another day, and I'll be going back early tomorrow morning. So, she'll be able to chill out and just do things at her own pace, though I'll rush home if she needs me. So that's pretty much our life. It's amazing how you can go from the penthouse to the basement in such a short time.

We will try again as soon as we can. If anything, it's made me more determined. Not too much else to report, everything was revolving around the bub, I suppose that's a bit of a void to fill.

We will get through it, and we know that miscarriage is rather sadly almost as common as the common cold."

I cannot explain the feeling of not being able to control tears. I said to a friend this morning on the phone that it's like someone has died. The pain is just a huge ache in your heart and you just cannot control the bursts of periodic crying. She said, essentially someone has!

I got up this morning after a big sleep and felt fine. I

felt normal. There was no pain and I was not tired and... I was not pregnant. Today is the beginning of the rest of my life and I've decided we WILL fall pregnant again and we WILL keep trying if it costs us every penny we have and some more, we WILL have a family!

So, I have now brought this journal up to date and have marvelled at all the emails Maria and I have written back and forth to each other. Many of these have been the same content as these entries.

I am proud to admit I have held it together until now, apart from a few tears when the bill arrived in the mail from the doctor's office. It was dated 10th May. I know exactly what happened on that date.

So, I'll end this for now and call it Part One.

I'm sure it will make interesting reading in the future as I sit with my children and grandchildren around me and think back to this horrible few days and remember how at the time I thought I'd never get through it… but I did.

Part Two

The beginning of the Recovery

Saturday 12th May 2001

Well, I can safely say that the pain is probably worse than I could have anticipated for both of us. It truly feels like a loss and you just can't stop thinking about it. I woke up this morning and Scott asked how I had slept? Well I slept great, thanks for asking, because I didn't get up to wee! It's crazy how sad that simple act can make a person feel at 6:00am in the morning. I pushed on my boobs, which had become almost routine previously and nearly always felt some description of tenderness, but this morning as I had fully expected, nothing at all. I don't even feel thick around the waist like I have which I don't know if this is just psychological or not. And as Murphy's Law would have it, we got an email from Scott's cousin this morning saying, *"Guess what? We're 20 weeks pregnant!"* It's like nature has the power to play a cruel joke on humans.

We've pretty much told everyone that needed to know our sad story now and it's just time for us to move forward. Sometimes it feels like we can, and we can move on strongly and everything will be fine and then other times a wave of pain seems to come across either of us and it's like we just can't move. It's all too sad and we just can't believe this has happened. Scott has been amazing through all this. I know he's feeling a huge pain himself, but he's been so caring and so loving, and has told as many of the people that knew so I didn't have to. I know he must be just as shattered as I am. He says it's probably a bit worse for me knowing it's all happened to my body, but I think mentally it's just as bad for him if not worse. Firstly, there's absolutely nothing he can do about it all and he must be thinking that if it wasn't for his 'boys' we wouldn't be in this position in the first place. Whenever I think of Scott I think how lucky I am to have him and how I know together even though it seems like a nightmare, we WILL get through this.

Sunday 13th May 2001

Well today is Sunday and so far, so good. Only tears after reading Maria's emails. As far as how I'm coping well, I'm not so sure. Yesterday was pretty bad. After having a good cry in the morning and Scott getting pretty upset as well, yesterday seemed to be the hardest day so far, we bundled the babies, (the puppies), into the car and went to Bribie Island, just up the coast from where we live. It's like another world out there and I guess we were so focussed on the puppies that we just looked out into the sea and forget everything back on Australian mainland. I really love it there. It's so peaceful and relaxing.

I had a cry in the car yesterday on the way to work and wondered at that point if I was doing the right thing. I got into work and our supervisor asked how I was. Big mistake and I went scurrying into the toilet with Scott in tears calling after me. Anyway, after another outburst in his office some time later, I finally relaxed for a couple of hours until most of the work was over and then got sad again. I thought I'd go off and have a walk in the cold air and that would make me feel better but instead I dragged poor Scott with me and cried and cried all over his shirt. Just when you thought you couldn't cry anymore!

It was a late night at work and it's amazing how much more energy you have when you're not in the first trimester. I didn't have a nap and still felt human and not mind numbingly exhausted like I have been, being up at that time of the night.

I'm taking the smart option today and am having it off. I've got today and the next two days to pull myself together emotionally enough to get back into society and continue my life. I think maybe I expected too much from myself yesterday and probably shouldn't have gone anywhere near work.

I even filled out a new uniform application last night for new pants and shirts. I had been putting it off assuming I'd just get maternity stuff so that was sad. It was also sad that my work pants do up again and belt fits on the usual notch. It's amazing how much your body really does spring back. Only last shift I was still leaving the top button open. I weighed myself at work and am the lightest I've been for about four years! 69 point something kg. It's so bizarre.

So today I'll just chill out at home and see if I can get through the day without any tears, and just try and take it one day at a time. This is *SO* much harder than I ever could have imagined. I feel okay at the moment, but it seems my demeanour is subject to change at any split second. I hate the feeling of not being in control of my emotions.

It is so right when they said as soon as you fall pregnant that your life seems to revolve around the bub. You don't realise just how much till something like this happens. I commented that we should have a holiday and Scott reminded me we were going to away next week to the south coast. Neither of us is looking forward to it as much as we were, and we now just wish we were going alone and not with our group of friends. I was just dying to get down there before and I think the reason was to share our extreme excitement with the guys of us becoming parents. Now I'm not fussed whether we go or not. I do think it will do us the world of good though.

Wednesday 13th June 2001

I haven't written for a while because basically nothing's been happening. We were slow to recover for the first few days but eventually picked ourselves back up and just waited for the next period to come along, which I might add, we're still waiting for! About two weeks ago I rang the surgery and the receptionist said it was normal not to have had a period yet and just to sit tight and ring them again on Day 1. She also said that if we were emotionally ready, then physically there was no reason we couldn't try again this period instead of waiting this one out and trying the second one. This obviously made us very excited and we have been hanging out for just the first sign of blood to celebrate.

SO I'm at the point today where it's starting to frustrate the crap out of me. I couldn't wait any longer for more information, so I rang the fertility centre, they said I probably should have had one by now and asked whether had had I had intercourse since the curette. I said yes, and they said there's always a chance that I could be pregnant. On the other hand, it could be hormonal, but I should ring my doctor. Bloody hell! I never thought of that!

Well, I jumped the gun and did my last home pregnancy test and it's come up negative. I rang the doctor's surgery and spoke to one of the receptionists and she's going to ring me back. She seems to think I should have had one by now too and reminded me the home pregnancy kits are not 100% accurate. She'd probably want me to go in for a blood test just to be absolutely sure. Again, it could be hormonal.

Once again, I find myself waiting, waiting... waiting... WAITING!!!!!!!! Wouldn't it be ironic though?

I should probably mention at this point how I've been feeling for the last five weeks. I'm still not drinking coffee but am amazed how much more energy I have on a morning shift and a night shift. I guess I should be more amazed at how little energy I had when I was pregnant. There is nothing much else to report. I am also back to eating more meat again, probably not as much as I used to but close enough. There is nothing else physically different at the moment. I think I have gained a kilogram or two, but I put that down to the amount of junk food I have eaten in the last week, it's been ridiculous.

Saturday 30th June 2001

Okay, since I last wrote it's all been happening. The very next day on June 14th and my 31st birthday I got my period!! How good a present was that? It was unreal! Anyway, I went off for a blood test the next day (Day 2) and another one on Day 12 and today it all happened again. Today is Day 17 and we had our first frozen embryo transfer. The scientist and the doctor both agreed it was a great embryo and had defrosted well and was already changing and splitting into cells. We're both pretty reserved as far as the excitement scale goes. I think we're both a little worried that something will go wrong. The stupid part is I am naively thinking that I've had my miscarriage now and this one will be fine. The bit I'm worried about is the embryo 'taking' at all. I think for me, it's the whole psychology behind something that's been frozen and now defrosted. Maybe it will expire or go bad or won't be as good as a fresh one? etc, etc. It's silly I guess. I didn't want to go to the toilet after the transfer today because I was worried I'd wee it out which is of course impossible. This is how ridiculous my mind is right now.

Anyway, I now have some more of those glamorous pessaries and I have to take them for probably most of the three months, at least up until the 11 to 12-week scan. Joy! I guess it's a small price to pay though. I have a bit of cold now too and have been told it's important to keep my temperature down and to dose up on paracetamol. I also have to take it easy. I'm thinking that means don't do anything over exertive and just relax and try not to think about the wait.

So, in my usual style, last night I worked out the days and the dates and I figure I should have a rough idea in about 12 days because that will be Day 29 and I'll be one day late. We'll do the pregnancy test again on Day 14 because I know I won't be able to wait any longer. I'll be lucky to wait that long as it is! I'm on a course for this whole week at work and off to Sydney next weekend, so the first week should go pretty fast then just a matter of trying to keep busy for the second week. You'd think this whole experience would have taught me a lesson in patience, but it's not made anything easier and the waiting is still driving me nuts! God, I hope this works this time. Pleeeeeeeeaaaase!!!

Friday 13th July 2001

Today is technically Friday 13th. It's 27 minutes past midnight and Friday the 13th means Day 30. It also means that I'm now four days late being due on the 26th. I have just been to the toilet and guess what? My dreams appear to have been shattered once again. I'm feeling stunned at the moment and cannot believe that this is happening to me again. I'm a few days late, I've gone off meat, I was feeling so sure I was pregnant and now it appears that I am not. I'll go back to the toilet in a few minutes and make doubly sure. God, I was going to do the pregnancy test on Saturday to confirm my suspicions. I suppose I shouldn't be too surprised. I was never convinced that I could fall pregnant with a frozen embryo anyway. This was my fear right from the start and not so much miscarrying. Now I'm wondering if I was in fact pregnant and have just miscarried again. How else do you explain the fact that I've gone off meat again? How would I know? Okay, now I sound insane. That didn't make any sense whatsoever. I need to get out of my head.

Anyway, I'm now the only person in the world who knows at the moment and I'm not looking forward to telling Scott tomorrow. He's on AM shift and I'm on PM shift so I'll have to tell him when he wakes up and before he goes to work.

At the moment I feel like never getting out of bed ever again. I cannot believe we have to go through all this again. I'm terrified that my worst fears are about to become a reality and that it will in fact take us years to conceive if we do at all. F*ck! I just don't know what to say. My tummy feels all funny and I'm wondering if I'm too stunned to cry. I can't cry at work anyway. I still have another hour at least here and then the drive home with one of the guys who I work with. I must stay strong at least until I can get in the door at home, then I can relax and have a good long sob. I wish I could ring Maria now.

I wish I could ring Scott now. I wish I could burst into tears and be done with it. God, seriously! Why is this happening to me? We both want a baby so desperately and I just cannot believe that we're back at square one AGAIN. What if the next 3 embryos don't take or worse, we lose some in the thawing process? God, this means another egg collection, more injections, more hormone drugs, back to nutty Dalya again. I don't know if I can take it all over again.

I'm wondering now, "*Why me?*", "*Why us?*", "*It's not fair!*", and all the other cliché things you say when you can't believe that you haven't gotten what you want yet AGAIN. How many times are we supposed to try this? Will we ever fall pregnant? I'm scared to voice my thoughts at the moment to Scott as I don't want to upset him, but I can only imagine that he'll be feeling the same way, so I should speak up, so he doesn't feel alone.

What if we never have kids? We just cannot afford to adopt. F*ck, we live in this huge beautiful house and I cannot believe the prospect of never filling those rooms.

I feel like there's a lump in my throat. I feel sick. I feel scared. I wish I could cuddle up and cry my little heart out. This is just so unfair. We are not horrible people and it's so unfair that the one thing we wish for more than anything is to have a baby and we cannot have one. I suppose I'm being a bit melodramatic but I want this so very much I don't know what else I have to do. In reality, this is only our second try and many women go years trying and never have kids. I guess I'd just hoped after the last miscarriage that this one would take, and we would carry this bub to term. I *SO* hoped this would be the one. I can't believe this is not the one. I cannot believe that we're going to have to play this game all over again in seventeen or so days. Someone tell me this is not happening and that it's just spotting and, in my imagination, and that everything will be fine, and we are actually pregnant.

Maybe we should put two eggs back next time? I'll have to discuss this with Scott. This has to give us a better chance than just one and to hell with it, if we have twins we'll manage. Thousands of parents do. Maybe this is the answer. Thinking this through though, I really don't want twins, although the flipside is I really do want a baby and I'll do almost anything to have one. If it means taking a chance with twins, then so be it. If twins are the worst thing that happens then that's pretty great. This will leave one or no embryo's left though. God, I don't know what to do.

I think I will go now and sit in my stunned state and wish the night away, so I can be home with Scott. I'm so very lucky to have him. I hope he realises how much he means to me and how much I really love him.

Sunday 15th July 2001

Well, I'm back again. I am not any more confident or any stronger but definitely more prepared, having survived another blow to our baby making project.

We've discussed babies and the lack of ours a lot the last few days and have made a big decision. We're going to go for broke and go for twins next time. It's a little scary but as Maria says, if we've never had just one baby we won't know any better and the next one, yeah right, will be much easier if we only have one. Anyway, I'm getting a bit excited at the thought of having two little beautiful babies. At the moment Maria is the only one we've told about the idea of twins and we'll keep it at that I think until we're confirmed pregnant and can confirm twins.

I have thought this through and I guess the worst-case scenario is we lose one and are left with only one. Well, in actual fact, worst case scenario is we lose them both. I don't think we're going to be that lucky with all three defrosting successfully, so this is really our last chance before embarking back on the drugs again. I don't even want to think about that right now. Focus positively and focus on twins. Now that I'm starting to get over the sadness of this one not taking and the more I think about twins, the less worried I am about having two babies at the same time. I'm thinking of the miracle it will be if we carry them both healthily to term. The miracle if we keep them both to start with I guess. Anyway, that will be round three and I'm hoping for it to start again on or around Day 17 like last month.

I know I've said all along that I really didn't want twins but when faced with the prospect of not having any children, God, I'll take triplets if that's what it takes! We just really want a baby and if it meant that we only got one, we'd happily settle for that too.

Anyway, that's the quick update, I'm sure I'll write

again in the next two weeks when it's all happening again, if not before.

Tuesday, 24th July 2001

Well, as she does so well, Mother Nature has once again played a joke on Scott and myself and has changed the goalposts. After getting a blood test this morning Day 12, it was revealed that I have missed my chance for this month!!! Apparently, I ovulated early this month and it hasn't happened in the last twenty-four hrs which means that it would have been a waste of eggs to put any back.

F*ck F*ck F*ck F*ck F*ck!!! In addition to this, I was told to expect a very short cycle this month, like expect a period at the end of this week or early next week! This is unbelievable. Last month I was nearly a week late, this month I'm days early and will probably end up having the shortest cycle ever in history. I'm only Day 12 today and the end of the week is only four days away!

So, once again, we go back to the drawing board. I cannot believe this is happening to us! We've been playing this fertility game now since about December '99, that's over 18 months and trying to fall pregnant for months before that and I have to say now it's starting to get a little frustrating. First the AIH (artificial insemination) doesn't work after about five months' worth, then we finally do the IVF and fall pregnant and then miscarry. Then the egg doesn't take, now we miss ovulation altogether. When does it end? Surprisingly enough, in this moment I'm okay with all this. I am definitely a little frustrated but more shaking my head in disbelief. If it wasn't so frustrating and ridiculous it would be funny!

As Scott says the only positive he can see is that we have a month off and don't have an agonising wait to see if we are or if we aren't. I suppose if there is any positive side, this has to be it, eh?

I tell you what, this little bub, (when it finally does come along), sorry, these little bubs, will never know how much we were desperate to have them, and the hassle and frustration we went through. I don't like using the word hassle here, but you know what I mean. It feels like we've gone through hell to have them. I think the journal will be an interesting one to read in a couple of years' time. God, it feels like by the time I finish it, it'll be over a thousand pages long at the rate we're going. Scott assures me that in two years' time he'll be cursing his kids and whinging and bitching like all the other proud fathers and all this will seem like a bad dream.

I mean really, what the hell is this supposed to be teaching us? Patience? Appreciation for what we have? Never to take things for granted? Bloody hell! We've learnt, we've learnt! Please give us a break already! We're going to be one of those people I've read about in the monthly fertility magazine, "*After nearly 3 years of unsuccessful fertility treatment, Scott and Dalya are FINALLY the proud parents of beautiful twins!*".

That's about all I have for now.

Saturday 4th August 2001

I got my period today.

Sunday 5th August 2001

Blood test today Day 2.

Sunday 12th August 2001

Blood test today Day 9.

Tuesday 14th August 2001

Blood test today. Day 11.

So, I went for the blood test this morning about 11am and rang the surgery when I got into work. Friday is the day! I know everything I've said, that I'd be sensible and all the rest but it's all happening for us on FRIDAY!!!!!! Bloody hell! It will definitely be the longest two weeks ever waiting for the day I can do a test. It just HAS to work this time.

Apparently as long as I went in before 12 midday, they could get the results back by 3:00pm so I didn't have to do a late shift last night and then get up at 6:00am this morning. I am much happier with a bit of extra sleep. So, the current situation is this... we have three separate straws containing three separate embryos. If we lose one in the thaw, we'll just thaw the second and last one. God that's really scary when I think about it. It just HAS to work this time. It HAS to, it really, really, really, really has to! I would absolutely love at least one baby before we have to do the drug thing again. Even to reinforce my reasoning that it really is all worth the stress and emotional roller coaster we're currently riding on.

I was thinking about everything this morning as I rode on the train to and from town and thought how amazing Scott was giving me the injections. I mean he didn't complain or flat out say "*no*". He said he'd try and try he did. He's no nurse or doctor and I was thinking that was a pretty big thing. And I was also thinking that Maria and Sam are both pretty amazing. Why you may ask? Great question! Well, every time I've been excited Maria has been excited with me and even if it's been nothing major. When things have gotten quite ridiculous or it's I'm just off for another blood test, she's still been there and has even kept track of my cycle! I still can't believe she did that! Like Sam, she has stayed interested all the way and when I've been sad they've both been so sympathetic and when I had the miscarriage, they were both just wonderful.

So, here I am firmly seated, seatbelt fastened, on the biggest emotional roller coaster and my ride length is indefinite. I cannot believe the high I was on, and to some extent still am, after I spoke to the doctor's office about the prospect of having another chance. I cannot believe how down I was when I had the miscarriage, when the embryo didn't take, and then when we missed the timing altogether. I think I'm emotional at the best of times, but I cannot believe the impact this IVF business has had on me. I know it's a major thing we're doing here but it is still really strange to have absolutely no control over your happy/sad emotions. I have felt at times like I am completely losing my marbles, like I am seriously crazy. Unfortunately, Maria and to some extent Sam have both been on the other end of both of these extremes.

EEEeeeeeeeeee, Friday !!!!!!!!!

Thursday 16th August 2001

I rang the fertility centre this morning to confirm 7:00am tomorrow and 7:30am for the procedure. They said that I could call back in the afternoon and find out how the embryos were doing and what had happened. I did this and was completely shattered when I got off the phone. Scotts Dad has been in town and we decided to take him to the Queensland Annual Agricultural Show. Stupid me, I chose the moment when Scott and his Dad were looking at the cotton exhibition, to make the call. I figured everything will be fine and I'd have great news. Not so easy. I spoke to the scientist and she said that they'd thawed all three and we'd lost two of them but the last one is a goer and has six cells and appears to be a good one. She said we'd transfer that one tomorrow and wished me good luck.

So, I should be thankful that I still have one, but I have this awful feeling that I'll get in there tomorrow and they'll say, "I'm sorry, but we lost the last one overnight". Aaaaaaaaaaaahhhhhhhh.

So, this really IS the last chance for this round and now I'm panicking and scared and worried that this one won't take either. I just spoke to Maria again on the phone and as she said, there's no reason why it shouldn't take. I have as much chance as all the other times. Neither of us can believe how crappy our luck has been though. I know I keep saying it, but I still cannot believe this is happening to Scott and I. It's totally F&^%*&ed! Anyway, I was shattered before and I think my brain went into damage control and I was well on the way to convincing myself that it wasn't going to happen this cycle. The more I think about it though the more I know I have to change my thinking and stay positive just in case it does.

I owe it to the baby to give it every chance and all my positive energy if you like, to be healthy and strong and to grow and survive. God, please, please, please let the pregnancy test come back positive and then please, please, please let me carry this bub to term and give birth healthily and safely. I don't feel like I want much, but I suppose it's all relative and what is a huge deal to me is probably not much to someone else.

So, I am still firmly cemented, riding on this emotional roller coaster and it is continuing making me feel completely nuts! I want to say that I just don't know how much more I can handle of this, but I know that I just *will* continue to handle it until I do get pregnant. I know I don't have a choice. I have planned my whole life to have and bring up a beautiful family and I'm not giving up on that plan. I probably should ring the adoption people this week though and just make a few enquiries. All I've ever wanted is to have a family of my own and this is proving to be so f*cking hard it's making me crazy.

Having said all that, Maria did point out in one of her emails that it makes the AIH seem like a walk in the park and I was stressed out about that, at the time. She's got a point.

Anyway, I know that worrying won't change anything and I know that I have to think positive. I know that I should just take it easy and wait out what is going to seem like two years and not two weeks before I can do a test.

I'm sure I'll write again either before then or at the time.

Until then...

P.S. The more I think about this, the more I don't know if I can get excited about donning the paper hat, shoes, and gown AGAIN, but I know I'll be just beside myself on Friday morning ready for another transfer. Once again, I'm so glad Maria and Sam are along for the ride.

Tuesday 21st August 2001

In case it didn't come across, I'm feeling a bit flat today. This baby thing is totally depressing me and having another crap sleep didn't help. Scott couldn't sleep from midnight onwards and watched some of the cricket. He was in the study when the alarm went off at 3:15am and was feeling very tired. He'd lay there for hours with no sleep coming to him and in the end gave up I guess. I think he's a bit stressed with this baby thing too and that's probably part of his lack of sleeping problem.

So, I'm not much fun at the moment and I'm afraid and I'm feeling sorry for myself. I'm feeling sad and miserable and impatient and frustrated and irritated and sorry for Scott and sorry for me and worried about Cosmo, our Labrador who is not doing too well. Basically, I am just plain fed up with everything. I can't be bothered doing anything and am trying to keep busy to distract myself. My brain is working overtime and I just can't wait until these two weeks are over.

Friday 24th August 2001

Well, it's been one week since the transfer and has probably been one of the hardest weeks of our lives. I realise that is a big statement. I thank goodness that we are both really in tune with what the other is feeling at the moment; otherwise I don't know how we'd have gotten through it trying to explain every outburst and every crying episode. It feels worse than any of the other "two weeks wait from hell" and this time it's really making me crazy not knowing.

Our whole personalities have changed this last week. We are such great actors when other people are around and when it's just us two, it's just trying to avoid the most important thing that's going on in our lives. Like a massive elephant in the room that we both see but have no explanation as to what to do with it or how to approach it.

The transfer all went well. Once again donning

familiar paper outfits. This time the scientist came and spoke to us again in the waiting room, but she sat down and started by saying "*how are you feeling?*" This made us both feel very uneasy. Anyway, she went on to say that the embryo had compacted, which nearly gave us a heart attack but quickly said that's actually a good thing. Apparently, it means that there are too many cells to count and it's changing shape. This is a really good thing! She smiled and finished by saying "*it's as good as they get*" and again wished us luck.

The doctor was very sympathetic and assured me that we still had a good chance and just to try to take it easy and not worry too much about it. She said if it doesn't take, we'll just start again. I have heard these words now what seems like a thousand times. Each time I hang on to them for dear life hoping and praying that it will be the last time I need to listen to them. I wonder if this will ever end? Will it ever be over?

Since then, Scott and I have avoided talking about the baby and have kept busy separately and sometimes together. I find us both very on edge though and we have snapped at each other at times for absolutely stupid things. I was just watching an Australian Soap Opera, Neighbours, on TV and one of the characters, Libby is pregnant, (of course she is!) and she felt the baby kick for the first time tonight. I of course burst into tears. It's becoming pathetic! I feel like a pressure cooker about to explode. If I do start crying, I'm afraid I won't ever stop. Yet, there's nothing yet to cry about. For all I know this could actually work. Unfortunately, we are getting to the point where I think we both refuse to let ourselves believe it, or at least acknowledge it out loud. I don't even think I'll believe it after a pregnancy test. It might just take the blood test AND the phone call from the doctor herself to convince me! I cannot believe what a long week it has been.

We work the weekend and have three days off next week which is going to make it that much more unbearable. I don't want to do anything, but I know it's best if I keep occupied. Scott continues to be amazing through all this and although I know he's hurting just as much as me, he's not talking about it much.

Okay, I'll stop now as I am saying nothing new. Just the same record playing again. I will write again probably next Friday.

Tuesday 28th August 2001

Well surprisingly enough I'm not writing for anything this time. I'm still waiting but thought I'd write a few lines on how the last week and a half has been. I am happy to report, despite my initial apprehension, this second week has been okay so far. Yes, I realise it's Tuesday, and so far, I'm fine with everything now. I guess I'm not really expecting anything and if we do get a positive, I'll be very surprised.

The first week was like hell. Walking around in a daze not really wanting to go anywhere or do anything and there was just one thing that constantly occupied my mind. I seemed to be on the verge of tears most of the time and just couldn't see anything good that could possibly come out of this. Maybe it's taken me a week to get used to what is going to happen in the next few days. We will either be pregnant, or we won't be. If we are not, then we will decide the path we have to go down next, which in itself feels pretty major with drugs and all that again. Maybe I have just been trying to get my brain around what was happening. Scott was the same for the first couple of days, but I think he hid it well. We didn't talk much about it.

Anyway, today is Tuesday and something should happen within the next forty-eight hours if it's going to and I'm actually okay. On some level, I think it will be a relief when something does happen or when Friday comes, one way or the other. Overall, I'd have to say last week was the longest week of my life and this one doesn't feel as bad. Perhaps I am in denial, or trying to cope, but I can honestly say I think I'm fine.

Thursday 30th August 2001

We are still in the running!! Okay, now the crazy starts again. I'm starting to get a bit excited and this is not a good sign. I have to try to remain casual about the whole thing. Think casual, think casual, think CASUAL!!! Oh my God! It's the only thing on my mind today. I think I'll go home and go straight to bed and stay there until I know one way or the other!

I should say here whilst I'm feeling fine and happy and excited, I'm really pathetic when I'm in the toilet, terrified to look at the paper and then smiling and relieved when I do. Okay, that sounds really crazy. I just admitted I am terrified to look at toilet paper. Who knew this exercise could have such an extreme mental impact on people.

I just got off the phone with Maria and re checked my diary. I'm such an idiot. Today is Day 28 which makes tomorrow 29. I thought today was Day 26. That's even more exciting. God, that's really pathetic when she knows my period cycle better than I do. There's so much I want to say now but I'm just not game to say it out loud just in case. So, I'll write it all tomorrow, all being well.

We're putting two embryo's back next time, it's decided! When we do, I refuse to let myself contemplate anything going wrong. It will be twins! We're due for a break in all this sh#t and I am sure it will happen this week!

If it doesn't happen this week, I'm not looking forward to the waiting next time round bearing in mind the 'transferring of two' decision. I think the blow will be twice as strong as we could potentially lose two in one foul swoop. But like I said, I'm pretty confident - I have to be, and I'm sure we'll get at least one heartbeat, if not two. Obviously, I'd prefer two but am trying to think of it realistically. Anyway, like Maria said, I've had my miscarriage, now my body is ready. I guess the next long wait will be till the ultrasound at 7½ weeks to see how many babies I do have and then the wait between this and all subsequent ultrasounds until thirteen weeks. I think I'll still panic then though.

I'm glad we're going to go for more scans this time

round. I couldn't stand thinking I had twins only to find out at twelve weeks that I'd lost one or worse, both.

Anyway, positive thoughts, I'm starting to believe that a positive attitude has to help.

15.5 hours to go...

Well, as you can see with each instalment of today's writings, the clock is ticking away nicely. With each visit to the toilet, I get more and more anxious. My heart is pounding and I'm nearly closing my eyes as I try to peek to see if there's anything that shouldn't be there. I'm sure you wanted to know that much detail. Welcome to the diary of what she thought was a completely normal woman trying to have a baby.

I've just had a delicious steak and mushroom pie for lunch and loved every bit of it! I'm definitely NOT off meat.

I will read again tonight that part of my journal from last time. I know I felt sure I was pregnant and then I went off meat etc and I then got a period. This was different to the first time when I was actually pregnant, and I don't think I felt anything until the equivalent of next week or the week after. I remember going for the 7½ week ultrasound and was getting all symptoms, but I also remember going out for dinner with Dad and feeling great. Just a bit tired but nothing else. Who knows, maybe every time could be different? What? Wait! If every time is different how am I supposed to compare? How am I supposed to learn what's normal or expected, and how can I pre-empt? This is a nightmare for someone like me that needs to understand. God, today is taking forever!

Friday 31st August 2001

Morning! And I don't know if it's good or not yet. It is 4:41am at the moment and I wanted to get this down asap because I won't be able to write until later now. Okay, so I did a pregnancy test and got a big fat negative. NO PERIOD THOUGH!!! SO, I figure there are a million reasons why it could have come up negative but have geared up for the worst and I'm fine.

I figure I'm still in the running while I don't get a period. Until then I won't panic. I'm going to call the doctor this morning and beg and plead that she let me do a blood test today, as I would have had to do one on Sunday if I had stuck to the Day 16 plan. I was going to go in Monday anyway though. Hopefully she'll say yes.

That's all I have for now. I will write more as soon as I know it, I am waiting for the inevitable crash.

... The crash came ...

Sunday 2nd September 2001

Day 1 tomorrow and that means blood test. Naturally it's a weekend, and they're only there from about 7:00am - 8.30am ish so it's gonna be just a few hours' sleep for this little bunny tonight. With any luck we'll get out of work about midnight and home and in bed by 1am. The alarm will go off at 5:30am and I'll be out of the house by 6:00am and in town by 7:00am. Yes, this is excellent. I just can't wait to go through all this again. There is nothing quite like feeling crap all the time, tired all the time and we haven't even started the injections yet! Did I just make a joke about Synarel? Yes, I believe I did. I'm clearly delirious. That's what it is, delirious!

Anyway, I FINALLY got my period. Like I said, it's Day 1 tomorrow. I said to Scott I would have been completely beside myself if I hadn't had the test yesterday and thought right up until this afternoon that I was still in with a chance. How cruel! Anyway, it was a relief. I can start planning the next few weeks now. Day 6 injections start (next Friday) and Tuesday I refill my bag of tricks. God, I don't know if I ever thought I'd be doing this all over again. I'm still scared too. Even though I know what's going on etc. it's still weird. I said to Scott, I'm sort of scared about the egg collection this time too. I know I've been through it all and I know what to expect, but I don't know, it's just a feeling and I just feel nervous.

Monday 3rd September 2001

So, I think we're quickly coming to the conclusion that it's the Synarel that makes me nuts. Tip # 432, Synarel and sleep deprivation do NOT go together. It makes for a very emotional and teary little bunny!

We got home about 1am last night and were in bed about 1:15am. For some reason Scott's alarm had a mind of its own and went off three times between 1:15am and when my alarm went off at 5:30am. NOT HAPPY!! We couldn't figure out what happened there. Scott said it wasn't even set to go off. We normally use my alarm because I hear it before he does, but for some reason his kept going off.

Fortunately and unbelievably we had a laugh the third time it happened, so that was good. It could have gone either way! The poor doggies must have been totally confused! Anyway, I was totally exhausted when I woke up this morning. Crawled into the shower and forced contact lenses into my eyes and set off to town.

By the time I'd gotten to town I'd already had a good cry and walked in there a bit bleary eyed. My friendly nurse was on this morning, an American lady who always seems to be there when I give blood. She's seen me in tears on more than one occasion and is just wonderful. Anyway, she asked how I was going and straight away handed me tissues. Through the tears I blubbered I couldn't blow because I'd just had my two puffs of Synarel for the morning! "*Sniff*", she said, "*Sniff, tip your head back so you don't drip*". Oh my God, it if wasn't so pathetic it would be hilarious. Anyway, she is just lovely, and I was smiling again by the time I left. I got in the car and began my hour-long drive home again. I now had time to contemplate my life again, as I do sometimes when I take the Synarel.

Yesterday I'd accidentally left the full container of canine electrolyte powder outside when I filled the dogs' water before work. When we got home, Scott found the empty crunched up container. It was completely my fault and I was so annoyed with myself. At about $20 a container it was a costly mistake when every cent is now going towards this baby. Cosie is still limping too so I was trying to figure out what to do there as well and seriously wondered how we can afford to continue to medicate him indefinitely. This of course brought me to tears once again. It sometimes just feels like it's all too hard.

Then I thought about every time we seem to get ahead on the home loan, we end up withdrawing the money and seem to be back at square one again. Surprisingly enough, this concept did not make my smile either. It's a bit like "*Woe is me*" at the moment and I have to say I am feeling particularly sorry for myself. I am starting to seriously question what this is really all about. How the f*ck are we going to afford everything? I'll have to start living at work again. It's no biggie but not what I'd prefer to do. It is worth it for my number one priority though. Whatever I have to do, it is worth it.

Wednesday 5th September 2001

I just got back from Day 4 blood test and will find out this afternoon if the injections start tomorrow or some other time.

One of my usual nurses wasn't there today but my other one was. She has two children aged five and ten years old, or something like that, and they are both from IVF. She went on to say it was not by choice either that they were that far apart. It was good speaking with her. She really knows what's going on in my head and sympathises. She gets it. So, I will ring after 3:00pm and see what the lay of the land is.

Later on Wednesday...

Just a very quick one, I just spoke to the doctor's office and you just won't believe this. One hormone has gone down - good, another hormone has gone down - very good, BUT the third hormone that should have also gone down has gone UP!!! F*CK F*CK F*CK F*CK F*CK. Basically this means another blood test on Friday. My doctor doesn't know for sure what's going on yet which worries me slightly. She was quite clear and stressed "*DON'T DO ANYTHING YET*". So, what's the bottom line? You don't want to know the bottom line. We may not be able to do anything for this cycle! Apparently, my cycle is doing something weird again and they're not quite sure what. We'll know for sure on Friday.

I am over it. This is total bullshit and I'm beyond upset now, just totally and completely pissed off! I mean F*ck! Seriously, WHY IS THIS HAPPENING TO ME?????????!!!!!!!!!!!!!!!!!! BLOODY HELL!!!!!!!!!!!!!!!!!

Wednesday 19th September 2001

I have resigned myself to the fact that I'll just be doing this forever and nothing will probably ever come of it. I will just to learn to live with it and that will be normal... On the other hand, if anything did ever decide to happen I'd be pleasantly surprised. This is not meant as a self-pitying exercise either; I've just been too busy with other things to worry about what is not happening in the baby department. So, yes, in protest I have even stopped taking the Folate tablets. I just can't be bothered at the moment. I am still doing my sniffing though. I am beyond counting but can say there appears to be no sign of a period anytime soon. I'm not sure where I am in my cycle mind you, I think it's only like Day 18 if my quick calculations are correct. Who knows, and at the moment I don't really care.

Later...

Got my period today! Day 1 AGAIN!! This is ridiculously unbelievable!!!

Monday 24th September 2001

So, I read back over the last few weeks and cannot believe how I am still here. I seem to be coping without even realising it! I am not sure how I am still married, and I am not sure how Scott is still sane, unless he isn't. I also wonder how it is that Maria and Sam are both still wonderful. I realised I haven't mentioned Sam too much in these writings. I can only say I have had all my IVF conversations with Sam on the phone and most with Maria have been in writing. Sam has been truly amazing. She's absolutely the best sister anyone could hope for and I love her dearly. She's been there every step of the way along with Maria and I consider myself very lucky. I have two fantastic women in my life and I am very blessed.

So where are we now? Well, injections start tomorrow Day 6 and another blood test on Day 10 should give them a rough idea when egg collection is. Like I've said time and time again, we've both kept pretty busy around here. Cosmo has been going backwards and forward to the Chiropractor which is about an hour and a half each way but thank goodness his limp is nearly gone now and he's so much better. Scott had his wisdom teeth out last week and I have been on night shift, so it's been a pretty constant week all round really!

Anyway, we're both coping well, the Jabber is not looking forward to tomorrow but the Jabbee isn't fussed one way or the other. Sad isn't it! I'm not being cynical, but I just can't care anymore!

Saturday 29th September 2001

Day 10 today. Blood test. Spoke to the doctor at midday and she said to come in for a scan on Monday.

Monday 1st October 2001

Scan today. Everything's going well. Got to see my little eggs and she's happy with everything. Says we're a little way off yet and to come back on Thursday for another one.

Wednesday 3rd October 2001

So, something weird happened yesterday and I'm not really thinking much about it, but it will be easier to explain now than tomorrow when I end up possibly in tears. Okay, I've had a theory the last few months that has pretty much been proved by calls to the doctor's office and blood tests. It's like a gluey stringy stuff. I think they call it mucus. God I can't believe I'm writing this in here, I really hope this kind of transparency helps someone one day! Anyway, the last few months I've had this discharge stuff around the time I ovulate and according to books it's totally normal and it's a tell-tale sign to a female that she's ovulating. So, you know where this is going, eh? Well, yesterday it happened to me too. Now most months I wouldn't think about it, but I'm not supposed to be ovulating at the moment, that's the whole point of these drugs. The only reason I'm bringing it up now is I spoke to the doctor's receptionist this morning and very sheepishly told her. She said it could be normal and not to panic but it is normally indicative of ovulation. HOWEVER, she went on to say that I couldn't be ovulating because according to the doctor the day before, I wasn't there just yet and she saw the eggs and follicles and said I was still a little way off.

Anyway, tomorrow I could get some really crappy news that for some reason my body over rided? overrode? – whatever, the drugs and I have in fact missed out again this month.

On the one hand I'm not too concerned about it.

It's virtually impossible for me to ovulate and we would have to be *the unluckiest* couple in the entire universe for it to have stuffed up now. No comments here please, I'm thinking it already, thank you! Of course, the implications would be that we've done all the injections for nothing and we're really back to square one again. Ha! Oh well, like I said, I'm not really thinking too much about it as the doctor would have been able to tell via the scan what was going on and she would have been able to tell if I was due to ovulate, that's the whole point of the scan.

Thursday 4th October 2001

Well, another scan today and I must admit I was very apprehensive. Yesterday as above, I got the signs I've thought for the last few months, meant that I was ovulating! It sunk my heart down through the floor like I cannot tell you. My thought was Oh God, seriously not again. I just don't want to do this all over AGAIN!! Anyway, I was due to go in for a scan today, so I rang the surgery to let them know what was going on and would tell the doctor when I saw her. I took the train into town and all I could think about was the baby, the IVF, the injections, the Synarel, my husband, the disaster this was last time round, and anything else to do with this whole last few months of my life.

Scott and I had pretty much come to the conclusion that it was all over again for another month. I think this was to save ourselves being shattered again. We're starting to expect the worst around here and it's just another blow where we have to waste energy dealing with it and then start all over again.

Anyway, I sat in the waiting room while the doctor saw another patient and was thinking about the last time I felt anywhere near what I was feeling today. My mind went back to the day the miscarriage was confirmed. I had sat in the same seat, thinking and hoping, but really knowing deep down that the worst had already happened. Yesterday was obviously nowhere near as bad, but it did remind me of similar thoughts that went through my head as I had then prepared for the worst.

I remember thinking about everything that's happened since then and how horrible and awful and terrible I had felt waiting. As I recalled the moment I saw nothing on that screen, it literally sent shivers up my spine.

The doctor called me into her room and as usual she was very lovely. I did my best to control my panic and prepare for what she would say next.

The good news is that I'm normal, well in an abnormal kind of a way. My eggs are all still there and we are still in the running. I saw them with my very own eyes on the screen. Again, she says they're still quite small and wants me to have another scan on Monday with possible pick up on Wednesday. She reckons they're waiting for my usual doctor to get back! Anyway, my mild panic is over and we're coming along nicely. Needless to say, Scott was thrilled! We both figure it's about time we got some good news in all of this.

I've read so many times that most women do not enjoy the first twelve weeks of pregnancy because they spend it worrying about something going wrong. I never want to be one of those people but bearing in mind what has happened to date, I wonder how I cannot be? I have no doubt I will thoroughly enjoy my pregnancy, but I also know that at every scan I'll be dying waiting to see if they're both - wishful thinking here, okay.

Monday 8th October 2001

I had a scan today. Geez it was really nice to see all those little black holes, (my eggs). She said that Synarel is the thing that stops me ovulating and I shouldn't have worried about ovulating if I was taking it still. That's why they love it so much! Anyway, she said if anything I should be producing more mucus, (God I hate that word), as a result of all the hormones and drugs. She also said my tummy should be a bit sore and/or bloated too.

I must say, it was so nice to have my usual doctor back on the job again. Not that I didn't like her colleague, but she is really *my* doctor and I guess I have become comfortable seeing her for the most part. Anyway, she ended up giving me a jab this morning and said I had one more morning of Synarel, one AM jab and one PM jab, which was the Pregnol that would bring on ovulation. Woo hoo! Egg pick up is scheduled for Thursday morning.

So off I will go again, with my legs in the air and once again donned in a stunning paper outfit. I'm seriously considering having my own personalised paper clothes made if I'm going to be frequenting the fertility centre as often as I have been. Don't be so ridiculous Dalya, it's going to work this time - for my sanity it has to!!

The Very Happy Egg Carton!!

Tuesday 9th October 2001

So, tonight's jab will take place behind the locked door of Scott's office at work! Then that's that! No more jabs for me. Thank goodness. With any luck this will be the last time we ever have to do this again. I was thinking that no matter what we have this time, one or twins, I'd probably be inclined to put two frozen back next time. Yeah, I could end up with two sets of twins but four kiddies suit me down to the ground. God, I would be in my element! I won't tell Scott that yet though. I'll wait for a couple of years! Can you imagine? Finally, I'd have my house filled to the brim. Two dogs, a parrot and four beautiful kids! I'd be like a pig in sh#t! Wouldn't that just scare the crap out of my poor husband!

Thursday 11th October 2001

Today I had the egg collection. We harvested an unbelievable seventeen eggs and we were both ecstatic. Seventeen!!!!! My God, we will never have to do this bloody thing again. No more injections, no more anything. It is beyond excellent! We're not expecting to fertilise all seventeen but even ten should give us a good chance of making our whole family out of this collection no matter how many fertilise. I'm really sore and crampy today and am dosing up on paracetemols. I feel great though. Seventeen eggs! That's heaps of babies. Thank you, thank you, thank you!

Friday 12th October 2001

Today I was shattered once again during what feels like an unbelievable ride that I have been on for over eighteen months now. I rang to see how many eggs had fertilised and they told me only seven. Well nine to be exact but two were abnormal so they don't count. Seven out of seventeen!! Fuck! Really? Are you kidding me? I suppose I should have been thrilled to have any fertilised, but I was not thrilled. I was totally miserable and shattered that only seven had. I am fast losing perspective. I guess I'd been expecting a lot more and the anticlimax was pretty devastating.

Then as if things couldn't get any worse, they told me that we were lucky to get the seven as the sperm quality was pretty poor. I was gobsmacked. I just couldn't believe it. I burst into tears and just... well I just couldn't believe it. For the first time during all of this I seriously had to think about donor sperm. God, poor Scott, how must he feel?

Anyway, I gather they had to fertilise by microinjection, as in hand pick the best sperm from a bad bunch and inject each egg to achieve the small success they had. It was a terrible blow and I just couldn't imagine what was going through Scott's mind at the time.

Later in the afternoon I rang up again because I was worried and kept thinking we had lost them all or had something terrible happen since my last call. The scientist told me not to worry and to just relax, and that they weren't going to look at them again because it disturbed them every time they were taken out of their little incubators. This was a critical time and the less movement and adjustment to temperature they had, the better.

Anyway, later in the day I got a phone call from one of the nurses I know at the fertility centre, I panicked at the first *"hello"* and thought the worst but it turned out the scientist had told them I wasn't coping too well and to give me a call. She had said *"I know Dalya, I'll ring her"*. So, I had another cry on the phone and she told me how lucky we were to have gotten these seven healthy embryos and that this really was a good thing. I eventually started thinking that if we can just transfer two I'll be thrilled. Please just give me two healthy embryos. Even if only one takes, please, please just give me one real live healthy baby at the end.

Saturday 13th October 2001

Today we returned, for I don't know how many times to the fertility centre and got dressed up again and did the transfer. We had one great embryo, one good one and the others were border line as to whether they are even able to be frozen. BUT, we did have two to transfer. My stomach was still really sore but I was loath to tell them in case they said okay, we can't do the transfer. I spoke briefly to the doctor and she said that 50% fertilisation was normal, and she wasn't really expecting more than what we'd gotten. Apparently, the more eggs that get collected reduce the quality and if the sperm is also poor quality then that reduces the number of viable embryos to work with. So, like I said, we did transfer two and I have to ring up on Monday to see what's doing with the others.

I think I'm at the point that I'm numb to any emotion. I have two embryos in me now and am hoping and praying for the best. I can handle losing one but think it would shatter me once again if I lost both. Scott is talking about having a break after this. He says he's starting to wonder how much longer he can do this. We'd have to have a month off anyway to raise the money again if it didn't work this time anyway. I think he's sick of the whole thing. I just feel like it would be months wasted that we weren't giving it our *everything*. Having said that, the roller coaster is wearing us both down and I guess realistically I keep thinking every time, God, I can't handle any more disasters or bad news. I just want something to go right for a change.

This year we've now done 2 full IVF cycles, i.e. two sets of drugs, two egg collections, two fresh embryo transfers and two frozen embryo transfers. We've had one pregnancy, one miscarriage and one curette as a result. We've missed two months because my hormones were all out of whack and one month because I ovulated early, and we had to skip it altogether.

We have had three lots of two-week agonising waits from hell and I have cried so much I can't believe it. In the process I have nearly lost my marriage and I have seen it grow strong again and then back shaky and then strong again. We have been built up so high, with wishes and dreams and visions of excellent and great quality little embryos only to be shot down by reality and negative pregnancy tests and late periods. That is just what has *actually* happened.

The emotion behind each one of those actions has been to its extreme. There was the extreme joy, relief and connection at seeing the first baby's heart beat then the incredibly devastating sense of loss at losing them. I feel like we have been up and down and up and down and up and down, and the feelings have been a variety of increasing intensity. You build yourself up and think positive thoughts because you know it is what is best. It is much better and healthier to be positive for the embryo. You eat healthily because it is better for you and for the nutrition of the potential bub. You truly believe it will work because you know how positive thinking is so much more productive than negative thinking. Then, after all that you find yourself dealing with the pain of losing that baby, the frustration of missed cycles and the tears that flow at the first sight of a drop of blood on the toilet paper. You are overwhelmed with disappointment and the realisation that it's all been for nothing *again*. The thoughts of "*how can I cope with anymore?*" and the strength it takes to go back and do it all again and again and again. I am just so mentally drained.

When I put it all down on paper like this I guess I can see how Scott would want to have a break. I am sure we have been on autopilot for the last few months and perhaps our bodies and minds are probably getting so used to what we 'should' be feeling at each point that it is almost coming naturally now, without any thought at all.

I never imagined I would, but we have been one of those infertile couples that have cried and thought "*Why me?*" I've thought, "*We're doing everything possible, and still no result, why?*" I have cried just out of pure frustration. I've found myself staring at pregnant women in the street and thinking as they have three other children in tow, "*Why can't you just give one to me? I promise I'd love it and raise it to be a stable and balanced young man or woman.*" God, I've thought as I have seen parents feeding filthy toddlers a diet of coke and lollies and wondered "*Why and how the hell can you have kids and we can't?*" I've thought "*Where the hell is the justice?*"

I am pretty sure we have experienced almost every emotion possible. The pure joy and happiness, the disappointment and frustration, the anger and extreme sadness not to mention the loss, despair, hopelessness, confusion, excitement, apprehension, anticipation and the list goes on and on.

I think over the last eight months, I have thought everything that is usually thought by an infertile couple. I never ever thought I would and hoped I never did, but here I am. So today, I sit here and document all this because I want to show it to my children one day or just read back on this time someday as I lean back smiling and watch them play.

I still have visions of having our own family and I

guess whilst it beats us down each month with each new experience that presents itself, it is now something that I vow to do to make my dream happen. I will keep on trying no matter what. A part of me knows that at the end of the day, it's not the end of the world if we don't have kids and I still have my wonderful husband and beautiful house and gorgeous dogs, all of which I love dearly, but for us now I think it would come close to the end of our world. It's all I have ever wanted, and I just can't imagine our lives in the future without children of our own. I can't keep adopting the neighbours' kids and at the end of the day, they're not mine anyway. This is the reality despite how much I care about them.

So once again, I'm waiting for another sixteen days to pass and right up until that phone call comes back saying, "*You're pregnant*", I won't be satisfied or be able to relax. After that call, at least one hurdle is over, and we can continue panicking for the next two months and wonder if we're going to be able to carry the baby or babies to term, or if it will all be shattered again at the twelve-week mark!

Sat 20th October 2001

Well, we're doing things differently this time, we're not counting. I know it's on the Monday, but I don't know the days, I know if I let myself think about it for more than five seconds it won't take much to add up but I'd rather not. Hey, I might even forget the Monday altogether and miss it! Nah, there's not much chance of that despite wishful thinking.

Friday 26th October 2001

The closer we get to Monday the more edgy I get. I just want it to be over. I know I haven't talked much about it the last few days, but I have come to the conclusion that these last three days have absolutely been the hardest! Every time I wee I panic, and it's really pissing me off now. Definitely a time for white loo paper and nothing with a red print like the elephants I have on mine. What the hell was I thinking when I bought this? It's the kids print toilet paper and has different coloured elephants on the sheets, but every time I see a bit of red my heart sinks then I realise it's only an elephant and am fine again. My God, I really am losing my mind, not only am I analysing toilet papers but I'm actually writing about it. Okay, send in the white coats... yes, now will be fine.

So, I'll be glad when I know one way or the other. I haven't been thinking about it much lately and really am fine with a negative result. I'm pretty much prepared for it. Yeah, there'll be a few tears but more of frustration than anything else. I don't know how I'm going to deal with the tiredness, I can only hope that I am pregnant now and that the tiredness I've been feeling the last few days is a result of this as I was on the verge of tears yesterday I was so exhausted. Sounds familiar I know but as soon as I acknowledge it as a possible symptom, I'll get a period, so I don't want to think about it. I was talking to Scott about tomorrow being the day I'd do an early test. I'm not going to this time. Last time I did it and when it came up negative, it was just too hard to take. Plus knowing it's not 100% accurate either didn't make it any easier. So, we're just going to wait till Monday and I'll duck into town mid-morning.

Sunday 28th October 2001

I have just been to the toilet for the millionth time today and still nothing. Okay, now this will be a bad joke if I get it at this point. I'm off to keep busy now and stop thinking about this baby stuff. A friend of ours rang this morning wanting to know how I was doing and to be honest; I'm getting sick of people asking me, "How are you doing?". I'M FRUSTRATED LIKE YOU COULDN'T IMAGINE WITH THIS WAIT, I DON'T FEEL ANYTHING, I DON'T WANT TO THINK ABOUT IT AND EVERYTIME SOMEONE ASKS ME 'HOW AM I DOING?', I ANALYSE WHAT I'VE DONE AND HOW I'VE FELT FOR THE LAST FEW HOURS SO STOP BLOODY ASKING ME!!!!!!!!!!!!

I'm exaggerating a little I suppose, not many people have asked how I am because not many people know. A couple of the girls asked, but that was enough. Sam didn't bother, she knows me better, and won't ask until after tomorrow, thankfully. I'll just be glad when I get that call saying, "you're pregnant"! Then I can tell these people and they'll stop asking me questions.

It is now P minus 17-20 hrs and counting.

Okay, I think I've come to the end of my wait. It's now 11:41pm. If I was going to get my 'visitor', surely, I'd have gotten them by now. I'm starting to relax a bit, not much, but a little. I think tomorrow is going to be good news.

Monday 29th October 2001

I'M DEFINITELY PREGNANT!!!!!!!!! YAAAAAAYYYYYY!!!!!

Wednesday 31st October 2001

WOOOOOO HOOOOO! are my sentiments exactly, although after yesterday's excitement (or should I say Monday), oh my gosh, I'm so confused with the days at the moment and with Scott and I being on opposite shifts it isn't helping either!

So yes, it was very exciting news on Monday. After our initial reaction and we calmed down, we both sort of felt '*okay, so now what*?' It was a weird time as we were both expected to be preparing for what to do next month. This time that was not a conversation. There was no Day 1 and so we couldn't follow the usual path that has become so 'normal' in our household. We just can't grasp that we don't have to wait any more and are having a bit of difficulty staying totally excited.

I was speaking to one of the nurses from the fertility centre earlier on the phone and then again in person this morning when I went to collect seventeen days' worth of those glamorous pessaries ($48 worth mind you!! they're $3 each!!), anyway, she was saying that we really should enjoy this time being pregnant because if everything goes well then, we'll regret not living each moment to its fullest. She also put it into perspective and said, "What's the worst that can happen?" We lose the babies, right? Well, we've done that and survived and gotten through it.

She didn't demean it in anyway and said she couldn't imagine how hard it would be, but it's not the end of the world and at the end of the day, it's totally out of our control anyway. She went on to say, if there was going to be disappointment and heartache we should deal with it when the time comes and not pre-empt it. When you put it that way I guess it does makes sense! She is a smart lady. I imagine thirteen years of work at the fertility centre she must have seen almost everything possible and it has certainly made her very wise!

I'm totally and utterly beside myself with happiness that this has worked. And yes, I feel in some way like we sort of proved our theory of fresh is best too eh?

I'm also happy to say that Scott is slowly getting used to the idea of twins. He's so convinced he's not going to be a good father because he's never had a father around and says he doesn't know what he's supposed to do. He keeps saying he has had no example to follow and I think this is half of his problem. He knows that his input will be 50% more if there are two and is scared he won't be good enough. I keep telling him he's going to be the best dad, and it's going to be even better because of all the effort he's actually put into getting me pregnant. I mean he's been in this whole IVF thing too not just me. I really hope I'm getting through to him. I can only keep telling him that I'm just as scared as he is (well maybe not really) and that he will be just fine.

Until yesterday, Scott said unless it's one girl and one boy, he doesn't want to know the sex of the babies. I still say I want to know either way. Don't ask what the theory behind Scott wanting to know only if it's one boy and one girl, because I have no idea. Anyway, the nurse said to me this morning that I will decide in the moment when they can tell me and not to be surprised if I change my mind at the time.

I read the emails from Maria, and I keep getting tears in my eyes (and a smile on my face). I cannot believe it's happened! It's just so surreal and I guess because we weren't really expecting it, it's even harder to believe that the normality we've come to live in our lives is now no longer our normal. We can go back to just enjoying each other and not worrying about needles or blood tests or follicles or ovulation or day counts or elephants on the toilet paper! Is it any wonder I have felt like a nutcase at times? We can now just look forward to those fortnightly scans.

Okay, so let's back track a bit and go back in time to the few days leading up to Monday. I was weeing a lot, but I think this was because I was anxious to see if I was bleeding yet. I hadn't been feeling off as such, just tired but didn't know if that was the shift work. Having said that, I had that crappy day last week where I was in tears with tiredness maybe should have been an indication.

Maybe it was, maybe it wasn't. I never really continued drinking coffee after the last pregnancy and just had the odd one every other week. I stuck to tea because I preferred the taste. With regards to meat, yeah, I think I'm going off it but will keep you posted though.

I actually feel quite sick writing this at the moment, but I think it's because I just ate a huge bowl of capsicum, celery, cucumber, tomato, sundried tomatoes, olives, feta cheese, and carrot.

So, I have to get a scan on 15th November to see how many babies there are and then I will have fortnightly scans after that. I am also on the pessaries until the end of the first three months at least - Joy!

I also saw one of my regular nurses this morning at the fertility centre, and she gave me a big hug and said she was thrilled to hear the news. The receptionist who answered the phone on Tuesday had told one of my favourites and she had told the other. They were all very excited. Apparently, I look brilliant and they said I really was glowing. I said it was probably the heat outside, but they insisted there was a sparkle in my eye that she'd never seen before. I said that's probably because the sparkle was always overshadowed by the tears that were pouring out of my eyes!

The girls there are so sweet, and it was so nice to be able to tell people that will know anyway if something goes wrong. It was such a good feeling and I knew they were truly so happy for me. They have all said to make sure I stay in touch, I definitely will too!

One of my regular nurses is overseas visiting family

in November, she's from Ohio. She said to ring her when she gets back to tell her how the scan went. They're all so interested, and I guess it's a success story for them when one of their regulars falls pregnant. It's so funny, I just never imagined myself being a regular! I have to say it is nice to be though. They're all just so very lovely.

Monday 5th November 2001

Nothing else has happened. I had spaghetti bolognese for dinner, which was very yummy, and am still thoroughly enjoying meat. I seem to do most of my weeing when I'm supposed to be sleeping which is a bit annoying, but I suppose you get that. I'll be so glad when I get this bloody scan done because I'm still not 100% comfortable or confident for the most part. I know it's silly, but I think I have been nervous for so long, it's a hard habit to break. I have spent so much time preparing myself for the worst; it is a habit that kicks in automatically now.

Tuesday 6th November 2001

I was feeling like crap this morning, tired and just yucky. I crawled back onto the bed about 12.30pm and Scott and Cosmo came up about 1:00pm to see if I was okay. I was fine, just feeling like crap.

Wednesday 7th November 2001

I had a peek at Dr Stoppardts pregnancy book this morning. I am loath to look at it as whenever I have in the past, something has gone wrong. I had the miscarriage or got a period within 24 hrs! Am I paranoid? Who me? Nah! But... the picture of five weeks was pretty impressive (or was it six weeks?). Ah how I love that book!

Oh, I'm drinking a lot of water too. I seem to be always thirsty. Well not always, but a lot of the time. I've generally got at least one glass of water going at home. Does this mean anything? It could explain all my weeing I suppose. Oh my God, maybe I'm not pregnant after all, maybe I'm just drowning my insides and they can't cope so have given me a positive blood test?

I don't know why anyone reading this could be blamed for thinking I am a little delirious or perhaps a little too analytical!

Tuesday 13th November 2001

I dropped Sam off at the domestic airport and sent her on her merry way, but not before I got some toast and a cuppa in the Qantas Club lounge. I wasn't expected in at work until about 6ish and I was feeling very sick at the time and had to get something in my tummy. Scott said last night when I went to bed cranky and exhausted, that the first of the symptoms were really starting to show. I guess he was right. Today is the first day I've felt really off in the morning. I wonder if he was being sarcastic.

I appear to have a huge problem, if I continue to eat the way I am I will be huge and looking like I'm eight months pregnant with twins, by the time I'm eight weeks pregnant.

For example, do you know what I've eaten today? Okay, here goes. I got up and had a cup of tea. Then I drove to the airport and went to the Qantas Club with Sam and had another cup of tea and a piece of toast and half an English muffin. I came to work, and drank a whole bottle of water, well almost all of it. A little while later, I ate a small bread roll with vegemite, followed by two arrowroot bickies, and now I am having a cup of tea and a box of dry cereal. I figured I'm trying to snack pretty healthily but as I write this I realise I am probably hungry because of all the bread and cereal. This is not quite the healthy I had planned.

I might have to buy some dried fruit and nuts for snacks on days like these.

Okay, so this is really something I am going to have to watch. I know that the last few weeks' weight gain has not been baby, and just junk food and too much chocolate but from here on in, it could be either. I really will look fat and not pregnant. Bloody hell! Oh well, I may as well just shut up and enjoy it.

I'm really looking forward to this scan on Thursday. I am so excited and can't wait to see those little heartbeats. I'm almost scared to see them though. It will all be real then.

Wednesday 14th November 2001

I was thrilled to be reminded that Maria put on 5.5kg in her first couple of weeks. I think I'm going down the same road. Poor Scott, we'll have to buy a bigger bed if we're both going to fit in it. At the moment I refuse to buy anything maternity to wear. I plan to just go up size after size after size before I buy maternity clothes. That is just too big a step. So, I have decided my first 'pregnancy wear' purchase will be in January and NOT BEFORE!

So yes, tomorrow is the day. I cannot remember being as tired as I was yesterday, so I'm inclined to think, and hoping, there are two little people in my tummy. We will have to wait and let the scan tell us the truth. So, I have heard and read the weight gain for twins is incredible. I don't even want to think about it at the moment.

Maria reassured me I was not crazy today, telling me it was very normal for having tears yesterday. It's not often I cry from exhaustion, actually it's probably only happened two or three times ever, however I do feel *too* emotional. Scott says since about mid last week I've been very moody as well. I haven't noticed it much but obviously he has so maybe I have been.

Thursday 15th November 2001

Today was a day of real mixed feelings. First I should say that since around the middle of last week I've become exceptionally exhausted and the sickness has kicked in too. It seems no matter how much sleep I get at night or how early I go to bed, I still wake up feeling really tired and overall like crap. I haven't been throwing up, but feeling really nauseous until I eat something. I guess that's how morning sickness works. I feel like I've put on a stack of weight, partly because before I even got pregnant I was eating chocolate and cake all the time, so it is completely my fault. I weighed myself yesterday and was about 3kg over what I expected. I am now 75kg. God, help me.

Anyway, we went in for the scan and I had to first empty my bladder an hour before and then drink 600ml of water. It's not that much at all but by the time I got in there I was dying to go to the toilet and one of the scans had to be done on a full bladder. It was so uncomfortable. Anyway, I lay there, and the lady did the scan and... there was only one baby!

I cannot put it any other way and I cannot say anything other than in that moment, I felt shattered!! It would seem that one of them never got started to begin with so I suppose it's a blessing in disguise that I didn't lose it after I had already seen a heartbeat, I cannot explain the heartache or why I felt this way. Of course this instantly led to feelings of guilt and selfishness that I was not happy for my other healthy baby and I really was and snapped out of it. I have one beautiful little baby inside me.

We managed to get a photo of the bub. 5mm in length and a healthy heartbeat 125 / 90 or is that over 125/60? I can't remember. Anyway, the size was good, and she said we're spot on six weeks and four days. This confirms the due date of 7th July 2002. Scary stuff! Anyway, it was a funny day after that. I had moments of feeling down when

I should have been feeling up. Scott seemed to be okay. Perhaps he was a bit disappointed that there was only one baby, but I know deep down he really only wanted one anyway, so maybe it was a bit of relief. I really don't know.

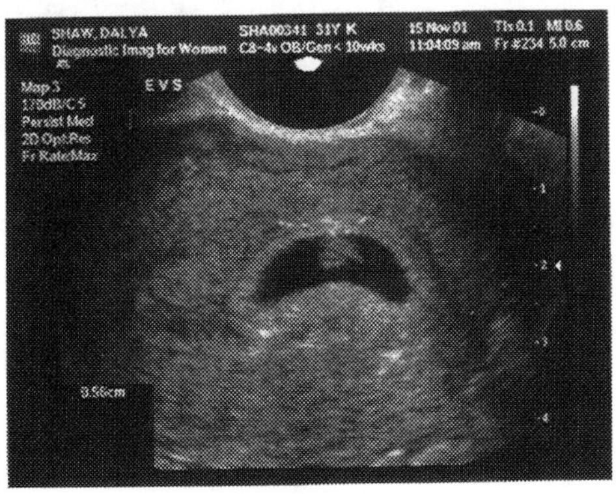

Sam reminded me I was probably better off with one as two babies were not two puppies and this way I could learn with one first up. Maria also said that she remembered just putting her head down on the pillow and then her son waking up screaming again. She was picturing me doing it with two babies and said it really was probably the best thing.

In any case, whether it is the best thing or not, I have no control over it. I have moments where the thought goes through my mind of "*we've lost another one*" and I don't have any more chances now to lose one during these twelve weeks. I guess in truth I'm quietly terrified that something will happen to this baby as well, and I just don't think I could take it all over again. I'm so exhausted and feeling disgusting most of the time and just don't want any more bad luck. I just want my baby.

I said to Scott, the most important thing in the world for me at the moment is to have this baby and if it means I have to have scans every day and then stand on my head for the next six weeks, I'll do it! I will do whatever it takes!

By the time we got home, I was exhausted, and I think it was mainly emotional and mental tiredness. I just couldn't help thinking we could be doing all this over again. It would mean that no matter what, we would more than likely have to do another round of drugs as we didn't seem to have much luck with the frozen transfers.

After thinking about it all for a while, well for too long actually, I did make sense of it in my mind and figured if something was going to happen there was nothing I could do. I just have to be careful and a part of me warns not get too attached to this little person, which of course is impossible and already way too late.

Friday 16th November 2001

I woke up this morning feeling like crap again, just in case you wanted to know. I went to bed at 7 o'clock last night. I lay there for a while, I read, I thought and then I slept, and I still woke up feeling horrible. I ate something earlier which normally works, but I don't feel any better.

I think the emotional and mental side of what I have done and what I am doing is what's wearing me down and I know I have to try to stay in the moment and take one day at a time. After all, I can't do anything else anyway. Each day I really am grateful, and I thank God or whatever this higher being is, for letting me keep this baby. I am told these feelings are normal and that my sadness yesterday was totally normal as well. It's the total disappointment and realisation that what you thought would happen, has not. Apparently I'll probably count days well into my 2nd trimester, sixteen weeks and four days, sixteen weeks and five days etc, etc. God, I hope not!

Monday marks seven weeks. My wish is to just me get there without crying too many times and my dream is to let me have a healthy happy baby in July next year. I don't feel I ask for much but would do anything for this, and I mean anything.

Monday 26th November 2001

Today was another one of those days that I wanted to cancel from my life. I was supposed to have a scan at 12:15pm but woke up about 8am after only about five hrs sleep after last night's shift and felt fine. It scared the crap out of me and my first thought was "*Oh shit, not again. Not again at nine weeks*". Scott and I had calculated when approximately we thought we'd lost the bub last time and it seemed to be this coming weekend somewhere between Thursday and Sunday. I was in two minds about telling Scott but I think I gave it away when he asked how I was feeling and I burst into tears and said "fine". I couldn't stop crying and he was in tears too. I just couldn't believe it was happening all over again. I was totally shattered. Scott sent me upstairs to shower and rang the doctor and explained the situation. She said to come in straight away and they'd squeeze me in.

I managed to stop crying about half way there but started up again just as we walked in the surgery door. I had only been sitting waiting for about two minutes crying into my tissues and the doctor called me in straight away. She asked what had happened and I couldn't tell her. Scott said nothing had actually happened, but I'd lost all my symptoms overnight again and I was panicking after what had happened last time. She was so amazing and sympathetic, and I got up on the table for the dreaded scan once again. I could see Scott was doing his best not to lose it, but he was obviously very upset. I lay there ever so still and cried silently, and I cannot describe my elation when I saw that little heartbeat beating away!

The tears started again, and Scott's eyes welled up too. Our baby was fine! The doctor said it looked great and the heart beat was strong. She said the head was starting to come away from the body and little buds were forming where arms and legs would grow. I couldn't stop crying. I was so happy and so relieved as I had been fully expecting to be in hospital getting another curette the next day.

It's hard to explain the swing of the intensity of your emotions when you go from pure anxiety and panic when you think you've lost your baby and then the feeling of pure elation when you see that beautiful blob with a heartbeat on the screen. Nothing about this IVF is easy. Nothing about having a baby this way is easy. The roller coaster you ride on is one of the strongest emotional experiences I could imagine ever having to go through. I mean you would think that a day off with no symptoms, without the constant nausea and the sore breasts would be welcomed. In my experience it is quite the opposite.

In fact, in light of what happened last time, it was the worst thing that could have happened to me, and I just didn't know how to handle it. I panicked, and I guess I fell apart. I remember crying my eyes out in the shower while Scott rang the doctor thinking, *this is all too hard* and *it's not fair on Scott* and *how many times is this going to happen? How many times can we handle it happening? Are we ever going to have a baby, or will we just be playing this game for the rest of our lives?* I was totally beside myself.

I think back now as I write this a week later and it's hard to believe that you can feel such strong emotions from one day to the next. They say hormones are amazing things and I'd back that up 1000%.

Anyway, we need to come back for another check up again next Monday after we get back into Brisbane and we can have another look just to keep us all happy. We're off to Sydney for the weekend for an engagement party.

Monday 3rd December 2001

When we got home from Sydney I rang the surgery and asked in light of my weekend symptoms, all present and accounted for, whether I needed the scan that day. The receptionist laughed and agreed with me that I could probably safely cancel it and just come in as planned next Monday at ten weeks. I slept for two hrs in the afternoon and then went to bed at 8:30pm last night.

I cannot remember ever feeling this tired or consistently nauseous at any other time in my life including the last pregnancy. It's like I go to bed exhausted and sleep for anywhere between eight and twelve hrs and wake up feeling like I've been hit by a truck. I feel like I am tired *all the time.* I don't seem to be handling the night shifts too well and I think it's all the late nights and the lack of activity for hours on end that completely drains me. I seem to be in tears most nights going home. My breasts have been so tender I can feel them when I walk. That is a bizarre feeling and the nausea seems to come and go and varies in degrees of intensity.

I can't believe I am saying this, but I really will be so happy when this part is over. I'm hoping in the next three weeks or so I should start to feel better. At least I know the baby is fine and I am obviously still pregnant.

Tuesday 4th December 2001

I am just filling in some details here from last few days that I left out before. We got a message last week saying that our usual doctor would not be in the office on Monday (yesterday) and we'd have to reschedule the scan for today. I left Brisbane on Wednesday for a couple of days in Sydney where I was able to spend a few days with Sam which was so great and then Friday with Maria. I got very spoilt and got heaps of presents which I was not expecting at all. Maria had embroidered a towel for Prawn, our new nickname for bubs in light of the first scan. I think bub looked just like a little prawn. Anyway, the towel had little puppy dogs on it and was seriously cute. She had also made a couple of different covers for the stroller to keep the sun out. They are also gorgeous. I also got a little baby hat, a Paddington Bear outfit, and a tiny snoopy pants and top set.

I met her friend as well, the one she's always going on about and she'd bought us a toy for the baby too. It's a fish with different textured fins and a spinning thing in the middle. If you shake the whole thing it rattles. Friday was wonderful, and I did absolutely nothing all day. I sat around drinking heaps of water and snacking periodically for the entire time. It was very relaxing, and I totally loved it. The next two nights were late ones at friends of ours and I felt sick on and off but did my best to ward it off with food. My boobs ached most of the weekend and I was over it all and just wanted to come home.

Monday 10th December 2001

Just thought I better do a quick entry. It's 11:42am and I'm leaving here about 12:30 for a doctor's appointment. I checked my diary and my next scan is not for two and a half weeks, the 28th December. Scary, I don't know if I'm ready to go for that long. How the hell will I know for sure that everything is okay? Oh well, I suppose every other woman is fine waiting that long between scans, I will be too.

I was also thinking, is it possible I have actually gone off chocolate without even realising it? I've only had one Peppermint Crisp, half a Milo bar, and some Almond

Rocha with Maria ever since I found out I was pregnant. Now that is a sad state of affairs! I suppose it's better than craving it. Maria says by the time I'm nine months, I'll have an intravenous drip pumping pure Tim Tam chocolate biscuits into me.

Anyway, I'm very much looking forward to today's scan. Hopefully we'll be able to see heaps.

I was up three times before midnight and again at 2am. The alarm went off at 3:15am and I wonder why I am tired. That's five times during a less than seven-hour period and it's not like I was drinking all through the night either. Each time I woke up I couldn't believe it and was sitting there thinking this is ridiculous!! Bring on the 7th of July I say.

10 Weeks today!! HOW EXCITING IS THIS????
WOOOOOO HOOOOOO

Tuesday 11th December

Yesterday I tried not to drink too much in the afternoon and evening. We had a very early dinner about 5pm and I had a big glass of water with that but just mouthfuls here and there after that. We went to bed about 7:15pm totally wrecked and I only got up twice I think during the night. My boobs don't ache like they did but are definitely tender to press, which I feel the need to do a couple of times a day, just to make sure they're still there I guess!? I can't believe how ridiculous that sounds.

The nausea is almost totally gone but went gradually

this time which was good. It didn't scare me like last time except for last Monday. I still get the odd blah feeling on and off but nowhere near like I was before. The tiredness seems to be a little better too in the last two to three days but maybe that's because I've been busy and then gone straight to bed. I'm not tired to the point of tears anymore which is probably the best way to describe it, so it's all good.

So, I've thought on and off about yesterday's scan and I still can't believe what I saw. It was just *so* amazing. Seeing that little bub bouncing around was just... wow, totally unbelievable. I guess it confirmed that I'm definitely, totally, positively, no question about it, pregnant. It was a really good feeling and I don't think I haven't taken my hands off my belly since.

I seem to remember reading in Dr Stoppards book that from about fourteen weeks they recognise and can respond to touch, I'm pretty sure it was about this time. The mother can't feel it, but bubs can. My God, it's all really happening. One of my girlfriends is itching for me to start buying baby stuff but I reminded her yesterday my rule is nothing till January.

I have modified this since by saying I will start in the after-Christmas sales which she reminded me begin on Dec 26th. I suppose I can live with that and I may as well pick up some things while they are sale. I'll have to dig out Maria's big list of what I'll need and what quantities.

Sunday 16th December 2001

I'm already hanging out for the next scan which is going to basically / psychologically give me permission to start shopping. I'm hoping that they'll have massive sales on baby products, and on car seats and maybe even cots and change tables. I am starting to get really excited about it all.

In the baby equipment department, we have finally decided on a timber change table, over the one with the inbuilt bath and possibly one with drawer's underneath. I can always put stuff in the drawers and I figure a baby bath is only a couple of dollars and probably a lot easier to do in the bathroom instead of the bedroom. I can already see what I am doing here. My planning organising brain is in full swing and at this rate, I'll be all organised by the beginning of February ready to go. I'm thinking it should be a fairly simple exercise, this baby buying thing. The reality is, no one is buying us stuff apart from Sam and Dad, so we won't have the risk of doubling up.

I can't wait for Maria to get up here and start decorating and for us to go shopping. It's going to be so exciting. I can't wait for Sam to see everything as well. I have moments every now and then where I catch myself thinking "*Oh dear God, I hope nothing goes wrong*". I'm nearly at the point of no return as far as protecting myself from getting hurt again. The barrier is so thin now it's almost non-existent.

Monday 17th December 2001

11 Weeks

Sunday 23rd December 2001

I can't believe we've gotten to **12 weeks**. Oh, how I am SO hanging out for Friday. Show me that bub and I'll be forever happy! My eyes filled with tears when I read a line from Maria's email about "*next year, you'll have a little sitting up prawn - who'll be nearly ready to crawl under the tree and attack all your Christmas presents!*". How wonderful is that? I just can't imagine. My (our) beautiful little Prawn sitting up! And nearly crawling!

Wow! I just can't wait!

Friday 28th December 2001

I had a scan today and our little prawn is no longer a prawn and a very quickly growing baby. Bub is absolutely gorgeous! We couldn't believe it. There it was right in front of our eyes, first facing up, then faced us front on, waved and turned to face down again. It was absolutely incredible. We were SO excited. I was even more thrilled because I could see the look of amazement and happiness on Scott's face. I'm just so bloody happy that everything is fine. We are now officially out of the high danger period and can actually enjoy the pregnancy completely from now on. This is just so unbelievable! I am so ridiculously happy.

The doctor said everything is going just great. She gave me paperwork for the Pathologist to get the Down Syndrome blood test done at sixteen weeks and the paperwork for the eighteen-week scan at the hospital. It's all so real now. It's all so happening. It's all so wonderful.

Monday 31st December 2001

I rang my Gramma this morning but was only able to have a short chat as she had her bridge friends over. She was so delighted with the news and couldn't wait to tell the rest of the family when they get back from Israel in a week's time. She was also super excited and said I was very smart not to have said anything until I knew for sure and was out of the danger period. I told her we'd talk again in the next two to three weeks and catch up then. It was so great to talk to her and she sounded so well and so happy on the phone. I think it really made her day plus having other people there to share the news with immediately would have been awesome. I can just imagine her saying to them "*that was my granddaughter from Australia and I'm going to be a Great Gramma...*"

Maria says the tiredness will go away. I DON'T BELIEVE HER!!! IT WILL NEVER, EVER, EVER, EVER, EVER, EVER LEAVE ME!!!! BOO HOO. I am now TOO tired to be excited any more.

Sunday 6th January 2002

Well, I used to have three definite rolls of fat around my middle. Well Scott likes to say I have three rolls for three stomachs but anyway. So, I looked down and sure enough it's slowly disappearing. There is no longer so much of a roll now but a larger rounder belly developing. I guess what I'm trying to say is I'm looking fat, but I am definitely changing shape! Yipeeeeee! How funny is that!

Monday 7th January 2002

14 week's today!

Tuesday 8th January 2002

So, we are having a baby THIS year! I'm 14 weeks and 1 day and still can't believe it. The tiredness has died down, but I still have really tired days every now and then, mostly well but some average. I'm still going to bed really early, so I suppose my body needs the sleep. The last night shift nearly killed me, and I felt like I was dying by 9pm, and trying to stay awake till midnight to drive home was a total nightmare. Scott drove mostly but there was one night we were on opposite shifts and I couldn't believe how exhausted I was. Anyway, as long as I keep something in my tummy I'm not feeling sick anymore and as long as I get plenty of sleep and rest when I can, I'm doing pretty well.

I've had a few stitchy type pains and pulling sensations across my tummy, but the book says it's my uterus stretching so I haven't worried. It is a weird feeling though. I am told that I probably won't feel anything until about twenty weeks and not to worry. I may feel a "fluttering" before then but may not recognise it as the baby. Oh my God, that will be the most amazing thing in the world, actually feeling the baby move. How bizarre!

There was nothing too much to report at the appointment and she said she'd see me again in a month on the 1st of February. She reiterated that if I was at all worried about anything to just call and she would see me earlier. We are so very lucky to have found a doctor like ours. She is just wonderful!

Oh, the other good news is that my neighbour is pregnant too. It looks like she got ovulation right this time. She's worked out she'd be due on September 7th and we are just thrilled for her. Hopefully everything will go just perfectly, and our bubs will be able to play and grow up together. I wonder how her two-year-old will feel about not one but two new little babies in the street.

I've also booked in for ante natal (A/N) classes and Breastfeeding (B/F) class - again. A/N starts the 8th April and goes for six weeks and the B/F class is just a half day. This is all so exciting and still so strange. We're actually having a baby this time. Sometimes I still can't believe it.

Thursday 10th January 2002

Today we made our first major purchase, apart from the packet of Huggies newborn nappies we bought last week. Today we bought a car seat. I couldn't believe how exciting it was. They had a sale and we saved $46! It's not millions but better in our pockets, right? Anyway, we had a look at high chairs and strollers and it's all very real. I can't wait to go crazy shopping and I am so excited to have it all at home. I just can't wait until July!

Tuesday 15th January 2002

I started working on the 'return to work plan' today and initially I was a bit worried because I thought I would only be able to get about six months off on leave if I took it at full pay. After talking to a couple of girls at work, I got a whole tree's worth of printed information on maternity leave, long service leave, recreation leave, employee funded extra leave (EFEL) and it would appear that I'll be off until beginning of March with other options of the beginning of April or even May, if I take maternity leave also at half pay or if I apply for EFEL for 2003. This is all assuming I start maternity leave around 10 June. It was all pretty impressive I thought.

I've found I'm at a very yucky part of the pregnancy and I'm not sure I like this bit. The good thing is I'm not as tired as I was and I'm not feeling as sick as I was, but I'm not showing as much as I hoped, and I just look and feel fat with big boobs. I can't feel anything. I can safely assume I am still pregnant, but I wanted to look pregnant too! I am so impatient to feel something else too. Bring on 20 weeks or whenever I feel bub move for the first time. I don't know about these 'flutters' or 'butterflies' I'm supposed to feel in the next few weeks either. I have been assured I'll just know what they are when I do though.

Monday 21st January 2002

16 weeks

Today was amazing. I was lying on the couch and GUESS WHAT??? **I can feel a lump, a baby in my tummy!** It's down in the bottom of my tummy though, where you get the pot bit of a pot belly. I didn't know that's where bub would be! I thought he'd be around my waist for some reason, but he's clearly not. Plus, it's the only part of my tummy that's feeling hard! How bloody exciting is this? I seriously can't believe it. I was lying on the couch yesterday, poking and prodding and rubbing my belly and came across this bulge that was not 'pushy' and quite hard. I prodded it gently and couldn't believe it was bub! Bloody hell! *I'M PREGNANT!!!!!!!!* Oh my God, it was so exciting for me! Finally, some sign that I'm not just fat. Naturally I took a couple more photos yesterday for my collection. I still haven't finished the film though.

I joked with my grandmother on the phone this morning saying that bub would probably come out all poked and bumped from me prodding and she told me not to poke her great grandchild and was quite adamant

I should just look but don't touch. It was so funny, we were both laughing. It was another really good phone call all round. So, yeah, bub has finally shown some sign of actually being there and I couldn't be happier.

I also had the blood test for Down Syndrome today. It was probably a bit pointless as it's only about 70% accurate and not conclusive. Also, we are not really in the risk category i.e. 35 years old or over, but typical me I figured it was an option to do so off I went. It was nothing exciting either, all I did was turn up at the pathology place where they took three vials of blood and I was on my way. That was it!

Also, today we stopped in at the baby shop, and put aside a port-a-cot which I got for a bargain price! Then we went on to another shop and Scott found a stroller exactly like the one I'd been looking at with a friend just a week ago and for a fraction of the price. I couldn't believe it. It was perfect and the only reason it was marked down was because it didn't come with the box. How good is that? Naturally we got them to hold it and will pick it up closer to the time. I must say it feels like it's been a busy day all round.

As well as all this, we spoke to Maria for her birthday earlier and she's also pregnant!! How fabulous is that? So, there's now the three of us. I was so pleased for her. She was feeling pretty ordinary but was pretty happy too. She's due around 26th September. It's going to be a big year this year for new babies.

Wednesday 23rd January 2002

Well, Prawn showed his extreme displeasure at me brushing my teeth today and I spent the next ten minutes with my head in the toilet bowl. It's not so much the brushing that seems to bother bub but the toothpaste going down the back of my throat and when I spit and rinse it seems to turn my stomach. This morning was worse than ever! Vienna, (the German Shepherd), was most concerned as well. It was very cute actually. Can you imagine throwing up for the first time at 16 weeks and 2 days? How ridiculous!

I saw my neighbour this morning. She said she went to the doctor yesterday and has a scan booked for this morning. I think the doctor has scared her by recommending the scan particularly after what happened last time. The poor girl was in tears. God, I hope everything goes well for her. She wants this so badly and she's had a pretty awful time so far. I'd hate to see her have to go through it all again.

It did make me think though, how incredibly lucky Scott and I are. We are definitely pregnant. We now just have to get past that big scan, but in reality, the chances of something going wrong at this point are decreasing by the day. If and when something comes up at the scan, we'll deal with it then. For now, we're just feeling very blessed that this miracle has happened to us. It's funny how you seem to appreciate things so much more when you've really had to work for them. It's shed a whole new light on baby making for us and we will never take for granted what a wonderful miracle that has happened in us becoming potential parents.

Friday 1st February 2002

17½ weeks - Appointment with doctor.

Blood pressure was checked, and scan completed. Both perfect! I actually wasn't expecting a scan to be done today but figured while we were being offered it, why not. Little Prawn was bouncing around like nothing else. Very active and from what we could see, also very healthy.

Monday 11th February 2002

19 weeks

Today was amazing.

We went to the Hospital Medical Centre and **had our 'big scan'!** The doctor said everything is perfect! He measured bubs legs and looked at the brain and heart and everything is just perfect and growing at the rate it should be. We were so thrilled! Then, he turned the volume up and we heard the heartbeat for the first time! It blew us both away completely and I couldn't stop crying! I think even Scott was crying but I didn't want to look at him because I couldn't take my eyes off the screen. There was our little baby bouncing round, waving and moving about and it was perfectly healthy. They checked the nuchal fold and confirmed no down syndrome. They also checked the brain and the spine, confirming everything is growing well, and there is no spina bifida. Phew! And the final big news is that the sex was confirmed. It's definitely positively and without a doubt

. . . **a gorgeous little boy**!

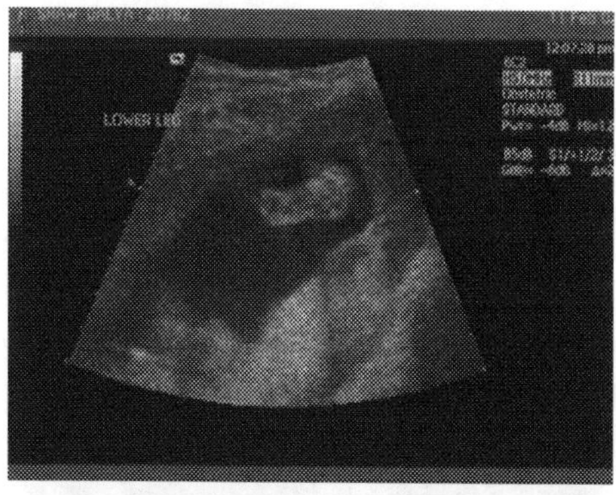

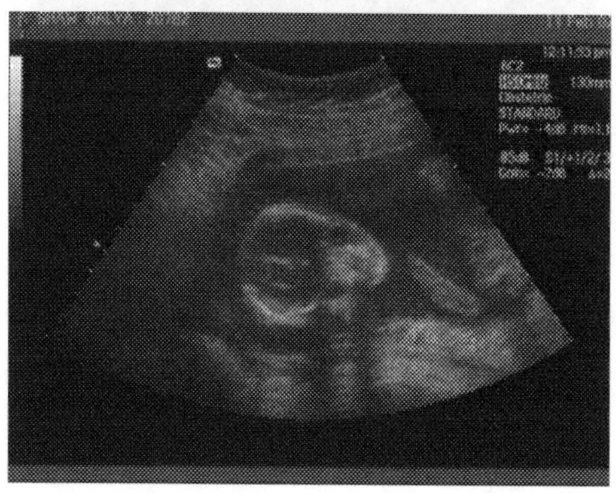

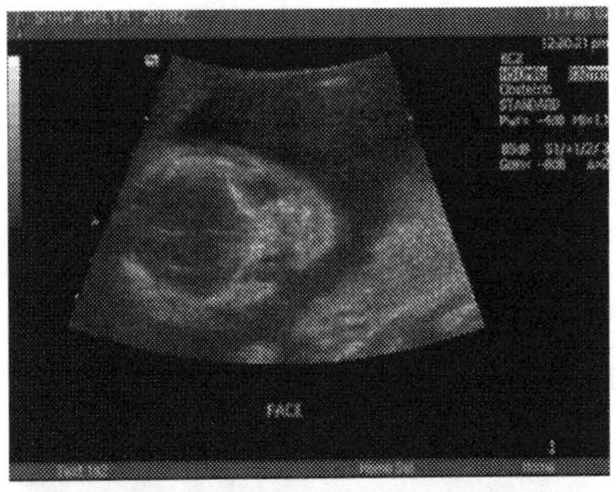

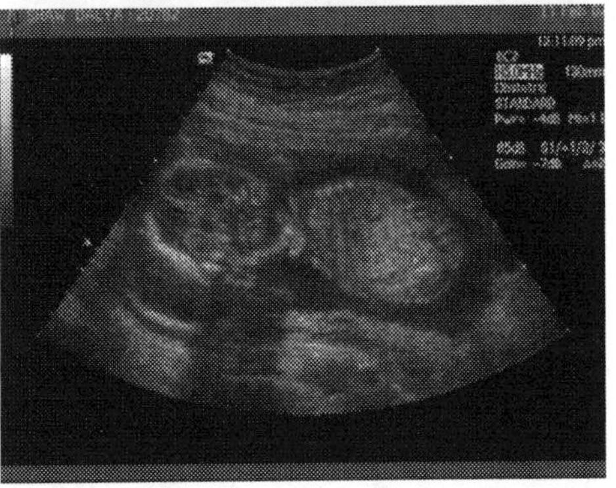

The doctor saved the above photos on a disc for us and two others as well. These are the third, fourth, fifth and sixth photo's ever taken of our little boy. It's never been more real than now. There's absolutely no doubt that we're having a baby! A beautiful wonderful baby boy!

Monday 11th March 2002

I think it's going to be such an amazing time during the first six months with Prawn. Scott will be there full time for two of them then part time; with shift work you may as well be only working part time, for the rest of the time until I go back to work. I can't wait to just hang out with Scott and bub like a real live family. I cannot begin to explain just how important this IVF was to both of us.

I look down at the dogs as I write this; Vienna is lying beside me and Cosmo at the entrance to the study. It's no wonder they are so spoilt, and why we treat them like humans, and fuss over them. I think it was a real fear at one stage that they would become our only 'children' and we weren't going to have any real human babies. I still call them my babies and it's probably the reason why I became so much attached to them and even missed them when I was away. I'm sure it's a very normal reaction and feeling towards an intelligent animal and at the moment they make up part of our family along with George, the Parrot, of course. Although I have to admit, I think there's a lot more understanding, communication and interaction between the dogs and us than with George, so I guess he treated a bit more like an animal than a human. Mind you, I remember before we had the dogs, he was our whole world. I still say a parrot is an excellent pet and can give you so much and I would never trade him in for anything. God, I'm really losing the plot here aren't I? I guess I'm trying to justify in my own mind, my over the top attachment to two dogs.

Tuesday 19th March 2002

I was going to start by saying that I haven't heard from Bub for what feels like a very long time but was putting it down to being pre-occupied all day yesterday and probably just not as aware of him. I didn't feel him much last night either or this morning and was getting a little concerned. It didn't get quite to the point of poking him to get him to move but since I've been writing this, he's obviously woken up and has moved around a bit so I'm happy again. He also seemed to have moved up slightly yesterday from out of my undies, or lower gut, to around my waistline. It felt harder there than usual. Maybe the journey wore him out and he needed the rest.

Tuesday 26th March 2002

Prawn was bouncing around plenty last night. You can sometimes see him on the outside now and it's so funny watching your belly move. Scott had his hand on my belly and finally felt heaps of movement. Normally he stops as soon as Scott goes near me, poor thing. Anyway, Scott was pretty pleased with himself. He was really moving and shaking too which was so nice for him to feel.

So, I woke up this morning and something happened during the night. I think I grew! I look huge now, well not huge but definitely bigger. I really look pregnant and couldn't be happier. I don't really know how that works or what the story is there, but I will accept it gratefully. I will have to take a photo maybe tomorrow morning when I know it's not food in there. It's been pretty exciting to see, and I couldn't take my eyes off my stomach this morning. It must have looked really funny.

Friday 29th March 2002

Bub wasn't too active yesterday and nothing last night. I even got up deliberately a couple of times during the night because I normally feel a boot then but nothing. At 6am this morning I decided that I had to know once and for all what the little rascal was doing and did a very naughty thing to get him to move. I lay on him! It was honestly ever so gently, and I didn't even know if felt it. It was just enough to put a bit of pressure on my tummy and thank God, the little man almost yelled "*get off me you idiot*" and has been moving on and off ever since. Phew! Does the paranoia ever end?

Sunday 31st March 2002

Hard to believe that I'm twenty-six weeks tomorrow and next Monday I start ante natal classes. It's sort of scary and exciting at the same time. EEeeeeeeeeeeeeeee!!!!! I can't believe we've come this far. Bub has been rocking quite firmly the last two hours or so, and Scott has had *no* trouble feeling him boot out the side of my belly. Perhaps it was that two-hour nap I had this afternoon after work.

Tuesday 9th April 2002

Last night was our first ante natal class and meeting in the maternity ward put everything into perspective! *My God* I thought for the millionth time, *I'm actually having a baby.* I think for all this time I had known I was actually going to give birth, but maybe thought of it more along the lines of me showing up at the hospital nine months pregnant and miraculously they'd present me with my baby. I hadn't thought too much about what I'd have to actually do to get it and how he actually comes out! Seeing all the beds and rooms and the whole maternity ward kind of scared me a little, or at least made me more nervous than I have been up until this point. I know it sounds stupid, but I hung onto Scott like there was no tomorrow.

So, I found out the following; there are plenty of single rooms, so I'll more than likely be able to have one. I think they said there were twenty-one all up and a couple of doubles. Scott can stay overnight if he likes and they will just move a trundle bed into the room. They also have a 'partner's menu' that he can eat from if he wants to eat dinner with me. It's all very exciting.

They also told us there is a nursery, so if you don't want your baby with you after 9:00pm you can book him into the nursery and he is looked after. I cannot imagine why you would want to sleep away from your baby, but I'm sure it will all become clearer closer to the time. In addition to all this, can you believe they encourage you to go out on your last night in hospital, suggesting somewhere nice for dinner and they will mind the baby for you? He would go to the nursery then too. I cannot imagine doing that, I cannot imagine being apart from him ever once he's here. I am sure there would be certain circumstances where people would take advantage of this, but I am pretty confident I won't be changing my mind.

All in all, they have a brilliant set up. It's almost like a hotel. The patients also have their own little facilities room too, so that if you want a cuppa during the night you can make yourself at home and just go to the little kitchen and it's all provided. If you get hungry there are sandwiches in the fridge and you can help yourself. I had no clue having a baby came with all these comforts! Each room has a phone and TV as well. I thought it was great and was very impressed.

The babies wear hospital clothes until you go home, unless you want to dress them in their own clothes before then. They encouraged us to make the most of the hospital clothes though as it cuts down on washing for the new parents, so that's what most people do. It now makes sense why the 'going home outfit' is so special. They also give you a stack of disposable nappies when you have the baby and you keep what you don't use in the hospital. It is generally more than enough for your stay. Very good!

There are a couple of bath areas and I found out they make you bath the baby every day, so you get used to it and can do it alone when you go home. They've got linen rooms where you help yourself to linen and clothes for you or the baby, well the clothes are for the baby, extra linen for both of you, and three big laundry bins. It's divided into baby linen and nappies, bed linen and patient linen. It's all very much organised and I was really surprised.

The theory part was very interesting, and we went through the anatomy and where everything is and what role it plays. I learnt a few bits of jargon, and some buzz words, and we even got to see 'the video'. Oh wow! That was very, very surreal. It was a text book pregnancy like Maria said it would be and the video didn't last long but was very interesting seeing it all stretch and the top of the baby's head coming out and exactly what it looks like. I think that's called 'crowning'. It was fascinating and really amazing stuff. Once again, I couldn't believe it.

By the time we left the hospital we were both a bit stunned and didn't say much on the way home. It is hugely exciting! This is really going to happen! I mean it's really real! We're having a baby!

Sunday 14th April 2002

Maria tells me it only takes about twenty-four hours to stop being 'scared' of your baby. I would have thought it would take a lot longer.

After reading about Braxton hicks earlier, I'm pretty sure I haven't felt anything either. I am sure this is not a bad thing. I am happy to report my breasts haven't leaked either and apparently lots of other women's do, so maybe it's not going to happen for me. I have felt what I would describe as a tightening, but not across my whole belly and just in sections, so I'm guessing it's Prawn. And yes, I still do believe he will just flow out comfortably without any pain.

Tuesday 16th April 2002

Last night's ante natal class focussed on the labour and unexpected outcomes. They showed another video and we got a run down on a variety of optional drugs and other ways to manage the pain. It was around about then that I realised I have come to perhaps a naive conclusion and I just don't want to know any more. I don't want to know any more details. I am very aware that when you have a baby, things can go wrong. I now know how to breathe and what pain management options are available to me and I know it's going to hurt like nothing else ever has. I just don't want to know any more new information and I will take it as it comes and see what happens on the day. How can you possibly plan for something like this when everyone says it's different and every baby is different?

I have not thought much about the actual birth and therefore haven't worried about it either. I guess I'm a bit odd, as everyone else I know that's pregnant has thought in great detail about the birth itself. I'm just enjoying each day as it comes, and the birth day will come too, and I'll work it out then. It may not be a very smart way to think about it, but I just don't want to know any more. Yes, I will finish the classes though.

Saturday 20th April 2002

We had a meeting at work yesterday with the big boss and a funny thing happened. I really had to concentrate on not laughing because bub was moving about in my belly and he kept moving almost like a wave under the surface. My shirt was moving, and I was finding the whole thing hilarious. Naturally I missed half the meeting and am not too sure what was actually said as I was much more fascinated and entertained watching my baby in my stomach. God, how I will miss this.

I have come to another conclusion in that I think guys get ripped off big time. I wonder why Mother Nature planned it this way. Guys never get to experience the child birth itself, so maybe they get off easy there, but they also don't get to experience feeling the movement inside their body of your child? I couldn't imagine how they must feel. I guess they don't know what they don't know. Sure they get the outside effects and can feel those kicks, but do they miss out on the initial bonding that happens when baby is still your tummy? Personally, I am not taking a minute for granted and am very aware that this is an incredibly special and powerful time.

Tuesday 23rd April 2002

Last night we had a tour of the labour ward. It was really great, albeit a bit scary. It was all very clinical, but the midwife was able to word it more personally and nicely. We were shown the bed that rises and drops electronically, the big balls to roll on, the peanut shaped ball, the shower complete with stool and we even got a peek in the door of the theatre room. That was a bit bizarre! Apparently, they have eleven people in there! I couldn't believe it! I'm still not worried. I have not been able to picture the actual birth as yet and am therefore not getting worked up about it either. Perhaps it's my brains way of acting like an ostrich? Who knows, but I still figure whether I spend time thinking about it or not will not change what is going to happen on the day.

I have saved the best bit 'til last. Last night we got to see a brand new baby. It was a tiny little boy and only five hours old. I had tears in my eyes and a huge smile on my face. I didn't dare look at Scott as I knew the tears would start falling down my cheeks and I'd probably look like a goose. This baby was so perfect and so beautiful I couldn't take my eyes off him. Scott said later that seeing him had really moved him too and it made it all very real to him. It really was a wonderful experience.

After our visit to the nursery they started talking about the delivery of the baby and caring for them afterwards. They went through how to bath them and some other general care. They explained how they might look when they come out and touched again on assisted births including use of forceps, caesarean sections, vacuum extraction, induction and I can't remember what else.

We heard the story of a woman who had a baby weighing 9 pounds 7 ounces, that's approximately 4400 gm! She decided to have her second child induced to try and avoid another large baby. She was induced at 38 weeks and incredibly it was born at 10 pounds 4 ounces, nearly 4700gm! It was unbelievable! The trainer and midwife said she couldn't believe the size and couldn't begin to imagine how big it would have been had they let it go to full term.

All in all, it was a pretty awesome but full on evening with lots of new information and we were both pretty tired by the time we got home. I think I speak for us both here that nothing we learnt came close to actually seeing that tiny new baby boy and neither of us could stop thinking about him all night long.

Thursday 2nd May 2002

It's been a good week this week. Monday night's class was good and the main topic for the evening was breast feeding. Fortunately, they didn't go into as much detail as the full breast-feeding class, but pretty much covered everything. Most of the content we now knew but it was really good revision. They finished up on what is normal behaviour for new babies and did a recap on how they look when they're born. We don't have a class next Monday as it is a public holiday and our last class is the following Monday. I can't believe I am saying this, but I think I'm really going to miss these nights. It sort of feels like I have been part of something wonderful that has taught me so much and, on some level, brought the whole experience that much closer.

Today I went for my glucose blood test. YUCKO! The drink was *way* too sweet, I guess that's why it's called a glucose test, and I felt really yucky afterwards. Prawn rocked around a bit though, so he must have liked it, or perhaps it was the opposite and he didn't like it either?

Wednesday 8th May 2002

I went to the doctor this morning and she said bub is doing really well. I mentioned the induction to her and she said as there is no magic test to examine the placenta, so she doesn't want me to go more than a few days over. She went on to say it's not like we're not sure when he's due, definitely on the 7th and there's no reason he should 'cook' any longer. If he's not born on time, on his due date, he'll be induced on the 11th or the 12th. She said that I'd have to have an epidural if I had an induction and wanted to make sure that was okay. I told her it didn't bother me, and she said in that case, "*let's do that*".

She also made the comment that I was particularly calm about the whole child birth thing and I told her what I wrote recently. It's not something I've really thought about too much and whatever happens, will happen on the day. There's not much I can do to plan if I don't know how it will pan out but was prepared and felt I had all the information I needed. She reminded me female bodies are designed to cope with the trauma that childbirth causes, and everyone does get over it no matter how bad it is at the time.

The other good news is I don't have gestational diabetes either! My blood pressure is still normal, I am in good health and I have a good sized healthy growing baby with a strong heartbeat. We are all on track. Yippee!

Tuesday 14th May 2002

Last night was our last ante natal class and it was a short one with heaps of food, although I wasn't particularly hungry. We had a review of the whole course in general, and we were given some Sudden Infant Death Syndrome (SIDS) info, and some after birth care assistance options that are available such as home visits and extra help if needed. It was another good class and it felt a bit weird leaving there for the last time. It was sort of scary I guess, as I knew the next time I'd be in the building, I would be having my baby. I think Scott was thinking the same thing because we just smiled at each other and said nothing when we got in the lift to leave.

It was very exciting as we all left with a goodie bag and I do love goodies! In it were piles of pamphlets and information leaflets and lots of samples. There was cocoa butter cream for stretch marks, and a jar of something called Bepanthen. There was also a Huggies newborn nappy, and a maternity pad. They are huge! – The pad not the nappy. Anyway, it was all very nice! I was totally exhausted before we even got to the class so consequently slept all the way home and went straight to bed when we got in.

I feel like my time has come up very quickly. The days are racing past now, and I can't believe it. I think I'm still quite small, but Dad says it's the angle I'm looking at it from. Scott agreed and said I can't see myself side on. I'm carrying really low too when I compare myself to one of my girlfriend's bump that starts from just under her boobs and straight goes out. I'm still nearer around my waistline and then I go out. We both look great though!

I haven't felt bub move too much in the last few days and it still worries me every now and then. I know really there's nothing to worry about I guess it's just become habit. I know he's still there and he does still move, I just wish it was more often. Maybe he's comfortable in a different position and I just can't feel him as much.

So, we're having a baby in just eight weeks. We're both so excited. I can't wait. I just can't believe it!

Saturday 25th May 2002

Yesterday we were in town at 10:15am for another doctor's appointment and it was really good. She said Prawn is looking great and growing nicely. I forgot to ask approximately what size she thinks he will be, but I guess that's sort of a stupid question anyway because I don't know if it has much bearing on his size when he actually comes out. I'm sure they must get it wrong a lot. Anyway, his head is facing down. How exciting! I've got his back across the top of my stomach, or uterus, I suppose I should be saying. So, if I look down at my belly I look directly at his back and his legs and feet are on my left side. This explains the boots I get on my left side that sometimes can make me gasp. Little boy feet!! We heard the heartbeat again, and again we were blown away. He's just so gorgeous! She briefly mentioned the birth and asked if I was panicking about anything or had any questions? I think she was a bit surprised when I said no. I know what's available to me and I'm fine with anything that happens. If I need drugs, I'll take them. She mentioned the big E (epidural) word and I said I'd prefer not to, but if it has to be done then I'm not freaking out about it. I'll leave that decision until afterwards when the pain kicks in and I actually know what's happening down there.

After the appointment it was off to the fertility centre for a quick hello to the girls, or whoever was there and to pay another $100 for freezing my embryos for the next six months. Only one of them was in the office and she greeted me like family with a big hug and said she couldn't believe how good I looked, even if I do say so myself. I really feel great! She couldn't believe how fast the time had gone and how close it all was now. She was naturally happy that it was another success story for them too, which I thought was really nice. The older receptionist that normally sees patients when you first give your name at the reception desk for blood, was also happy to see me. She couldn't believe how close it was either. It really is like an extended family there and it's funny and comforting how welcome they make you feel.

Monday 3rd June 2002

My dad says heartburn has something to do with the amount of hair on the baby's head. I hope that is an old wives' tale, otherwise I may be having a little ape. I have not been too bad lately, just here and there, but had it pretty bad again yesterday morning. It didn't last too long as I think I drowned it in milk again. Come to think of it, I've really only had about three days where it's been bad and have probably noticed it there maybe two or three other times, so I don't know what I'm complaining about! Other than that, I have been in good health and felt great.

Today marks 35 weeks and I am nearly in my last month! MY GOODNESS, I'M NEARLY IN MY LAST MONTH!!!

Well, Prawn has had a busy few days. He rocked around Saturday and Sunday and it was such a wonderful feeling. He appears to be sleeping at the moment though but I felt him a few times during the night. I think he had hiccups yesterday as there was a funny little pulse right down at the bottom of my belly that went on for ages. It was so incredibly cute. I am so bloody excited about this baby, it's keeping me on such a high. I still can't believe it's real sometimes and neither can Scott. God, in six weeks we'll be parents. We'll have little Prawn here with us. That's so soon. EEEeeeeeeeee!!!!!!! It's nearly finally happening.

Thursday 6th June 2002

I went to the doctor again yesterday and we had a good chat. She is so pleased with everything and she also said she can't believe how fast the time has gone. She said he'll be here before we know it. I was telling her about the news story of the thirteen-pound baby born in the United States. She assured me I don't have to worry about that as mine is nowhere near that weight. She indicated that she didn't want him to go over about eight and a half pounds and if we did end up with a big baby, it would be Caesar anyway. She just doesn't want to take any chances at this stage of the game but said he's growing really well and feels like a good size but not huge. The head is still down which she's very pleased about and said that he sounds great. How bloody exciting!!! I know I am repeating myself over and over, but I seriously can't wait. I'm so looking forward to it all. She asked again if I was worried about the birth yet and again I laughed and said no, should I be? She said no, and that it's better if I didn't worry. Everything should be fine from what she can feel.

I am getting the impression this is a big deal for women. Maybe most women are concerned about the birth, and maybe they do worry about what will happen. I honestly have not thought a lot about it.

I had a reasonably early night and then Prawn thought it was a great idea about 1am to wake up and he bounced and kicked for nearly an hour. It was so nice. It was like our very own special time together. A part of me would have rather been sleeping but I relished in that hour and lay there smiling with my eyes closed. I am having a beautiful baby boy.

I weighed myself this morning and I appear to have put on another 1.5kg since last week. That's ridiculous.

Tuesday 18th June 2002

I am now down to weekly appointments and have been for the last few weeks. I see my doctor again this Wednesday then probably her colleague next week, then mine again the following week and then that's probably the last appointment I have with her before I see her in hospital. I'm assuming I'll speak to her on the Monday or Tuesday if Prawn doesn't arrive on the Sunday when he's due. She didn't say much more other than the usual, I look great, and my blood pressure is normal, he's growing really well, and all looks good. She doesn't anticipate any problems at this stage and wanted to know if I was nervous. I laughed and said, "No, should I be?" Oh, and she definitely doesn't want me to go overdue. I still need to remind myself this is really happening. I think the closer it gets the more surreal it feels. I've got less than three weeks now and it's just so strange. It honestly gives me goose bumps just thinking about it.

I held a girlfriend's little three-week-old boy yesterday and he was so perfect and so little and so beautiful that I could have just cried. He has tiny little hands and tiny little fingers and the biggest blue bug eyes you ever saw. He is just so incredibly amazing.

Wednesday 19th June 2002

I had another appointment today and she did a quick scan. All we saw was this huge head, well it looked huge on the screen, and she said he's way down there which is great news. We are in a good position and everything looks great. She said she can't tell for sure but thinks he's a pretty average size. That's what I wanted to hear! She also said to wait for her, as she's now away for a week. I told her I'd be sure to cross my legs. So, I will see her colleague next week and then her on the 1st for probably my last appointment. Bloody hell! It's really close now.

Friday 21st June 2002

I weighed myself on the way into town for dinner with Dad and have hit the 10kg weight gain mark. I can't imagine putting on much more than that but will try to get one more weigh in before I pop just to be sure. Perhaps that will be on the way to the hospital to deliver! Ha ha.

Dad said that he thinks Sam was about 7 pounds, just over 3000 grams. He said Mum didn't look pregnant the whole time and almost up until the very end. He remembered he stopped into their local pub for a drink after Sam was born and everyone asked where Mum was, and he said she had had a baby. Apparently half of them didn't even know she was pregnant! He said I'm carrying the same as mum did, and whilst you could definitely tell with my white fitted white top on tonight to accentuate my belly – I am making the most of these last few weeks, even though I still don't think I look huge.

Monday 24th June 2002

38 weeks

Well, if all studies are correct than it means as of today my bun is cooked and we're just browning from here on in. WOOO HOOO. I've nearly made it! The first part of the adventure is just about done. I've decided too that from the labour onwards will be called part three of my diary. I had part one from the beginning right up until the miscarriage and all that went on with that. Then I started part two and figured that was an apt way to continue my story up until now and soon we will enter part three. In twenty years' time I can look back on it and think, my God, did we really do all that stuff?

By then they'll probably be selling babies in a range of sizes and colours and races in exclusive boutiques and technology will have gone completely haywire and perhaps IVF will be a thing of the past or phasing out anyway.

Wednesday 26th June 2002

As I read back over this journal for the millionth time, I realise that so much has happened in the last few weeks. There are also patches of this journal that are blank when you'd think I'd have written something interesting or exciting. Unfortunately, we lost a lot during a computer crash, so I've been trying to retrieve what I could from emails and memory. It's amazing what you remember and what you forget!

Anyway, we're now 38 weeks and 2 days and the last fifteen weeks have gone so fast. Staying busy has definitely helped but I never imagined it going quite this fast.

I finished up work on June 9th which gave me four weeks at home before Bub is due and I've been flat out ever since. I've managed to get some of the things done that I planned as far as organising and cleaning but not everything. Hopefully he won't come too early.

So as of Monday, he's full term and it's just a matter of waiting now. At least I know he'll be here for sure by the 12th at the latest.

Overall, I've had a dream pregnancy. I've felt great, only put on about 10kg altogether, I've only had heartburn half a dozen times and am still sleeping well and not particularly uncomfortable. I'm carrying quite low and not huge, so I think this could be why I feel so good. People can't believe how close I am for my size and I must admit I've felt a bit ripped off at times because I wanted to be this huge pregnant woman and I haven't been. I suppose I should be thankful and I guess it's a probably a good thing. I should be able to lose a lot of the baby weight quite quickly and hopefully won't have to work too hard to lose the rest.

Prawn is definitely more cramped than before, and I don't feel him as much but definitely still several times a day. He seems to kick mostly out my left side and sometimes he's quite hard and takes my breath away. I love feeling him and really will miss my big belly. I'm not wishing away this pregnancy at all but will be happy when he's here.

The nursery is all finished now and looks excellent. Maria came up the end of April and we did it all then. I just had a few last-minute finishing touches to add. I am so happy with it and I can't wait to have bub in there.

Scott surprised me with a beautiful 'Papa Bear' gliding chair to feed in and the accompanying gliding ottoman for the nursery. It looks so good! It was a brilliant idea and a great surprise for my birthday which was a bit of a non-event this year. I honestly wasn't too interested on the day knowing that my real present was only a few weeks away.

My hospital bag is finally almost packed, with the exception of my clothes, undies and snacks for my wonderful husband, which I'll pack at the last minute.

He really has been amazing through all this. He hasn't missed a single doctor's appointment even though we're now down to weekly visits. He's still blown away by the heartbeat and never complains about me grabbing his hand to feel Prawn move or the feel his hiccups. He's catered to my every whim and I know I am a very lucky woman.

He's so excited about the arrival of our first child and I am too. We talk about things that will change, how we'll do stuff and what it will be like. It's been so great having this time and these long talks with him. He gets up every morning with how many days left till the 7th and had even started counting hours, he's so funny. Prawn couldn't hope for a better father than Scott.

We're convinced the dogs will be fine with him too and have made a point of letting them smell everything that goes into the nursery. I think Vienna will be a real protector to him and hopefully they'll all grow to become best of friends. George, on the other hand, might be a problem but we'll tackle that when and if it arises.

Friday 28th June 2002

My appointment went really well yesterday. I didn't have to wait at all and she said I'm looking perfect. Bub is still growing well. He is a good average size for this stage. I asked about the engagement and she said she could feel 2/5 of the head, so I'm guessing he's 3/5 engaged! Actually, I am not even sure what that means! She said that it doesn't really mean anything as you can engage from six weeks before the birth to when you're actually in labour. It doesn't predict when you'll go but she said by my usual doctor's notes, and with all looking so well, it won't be long now.

After the appointment, I spent the next half an hour chatting to the receptionist. She remembered me sitting there at ten and twelve weeks in a panic and eagerly waiting for my scan and now I'm ready to have this little man. She confirmed that my usual doctor will see me again on Monday and then probably not again then until the birth. She said that she may suggest or at least discuss the option of having him next week as opposed to waiting till the 7th. But she agreed that she wouldn't let me go over. Goodness only knows when he'll be born now but I'm guessing sooner rather than later. I expect she'll let me go until the Sunday when I'm due and then book me in for early that week. How flippin' exciting! We also talked a bit more about induction and the gel and she told me that both her kids were caesarean sections and she wouldn't go any other way.

God, I can't believe how close we are. I keep repeating myself now, but it's really, really close!

P.S. I think I've grown again in the last two weeks or so. I look very pregnant now and I took a few more photos this morning.

Sunday 30th June 2002

The last two weeks or so, Prawn has been a big fan of pushing his feet out my left side just above my hip bone. It seems he was higher before but who knows. Oh, I am so going to miss this. I hardly notice him move much these days but after dinner he's pretty active and the leg stretching exercise is always a good one. As long as he keeps on moving, I'm happy.

Tuesday 2nd July 2002

39 weeks 1 day

Our usual doctor was back for yesterday's appointment and there is nothing much new to report. She did say that it must be pretty close as his head is way down there. She said to make an appointment for Monday just in case but would hope to see me before then in the hospital. We discussed induction and I said that I'd really like to have him next week if he's not on time. She tried to book me in for Tuesday, but it ended up being for Wednesday. So now I'm pretty sure I go in for the gel on Tuesday night and then Prawn will be born the Wednesday all being well.

Scott and I were so excited when we left, I couldn't get the smile off my face. I rang Sam and she was so excited too and I realised that she'll be up here on Saturday and how close it all was. I can't wait for her to be here and I am so glad she will have the first few days with him.

So, when I left the surgery, I was on such a high but by the time we got half way home I was crying my eyes out. I couldn't believe I was having a baby and I think planning the induction and booking me in for Tuesday night with him arriving on Wednesday scared the crap out of me for the first time in nine months. I think it was the first time ever I'd seriously contemplated him being here live in person and exactly how that was going to happen. The thought of being in hospital scares me a little, I've never been in hospital before. And now the thought of having him makes me nervous as well. It was around this time that I made the most ridiculous comment to Scott amongst my tears "*What if it really hurts?*" This is how little I've thought of it, like *not at all*!

Anyway, I was in a fairly solemn mood from then on for pretty much the rest of the day. I think it all became more real than ever when the doctor actually booked us in and it's now all ready to go, if he doesn't show up beforehand.

So then I get an email from Maria saying, "*if you start to get teary and feel like cleaning even more than normal, it's probably imminent...*" and I thought, oh sh#t! Maybe it'll be tonight!?

But as you can see, I'm still here. I vacuumed and washed all the floors this morning, nothing more than usual though. I did get Cosie's tablets organised though, so at least I know he's looked after. I also picked them up another fresh bone today for when I'm in hospital. I'm going to really miss my fur and feather babies!

So, I'm relaxed again and doing the ostrich thing once more with regards to the birth, but I'm definitely more aware of what's going to happen than I was yesterday morning.

I suddenly decided about 5:30pm tonight, that it was time to garden. For the record, I hate gardening, but I wanted to get the area outside the study window done and decided there and then was the time. One of my neighbours thought I was crazy and I'm sure Scott did too. Having said that, we got all the paper laid and the plastic over the top to kill the weeds and now we just need some coloured stones to be poured in and a couple of nice pots or even one big pot with a tree in it. I might dedicate it to Prawn seeing as it's something I have only just decided, and it does coincide with being just before his arrival.

Sunday 7th July 2002

40 weeks!!!
Due Today!!

It's 7am and I have nothing! I feel fine, I slept well, I felt him move but I did not go into labour. I have nothing else new. Oh well, at least I didn't wreck the new mattress. I'm thinking about putting down one of the baby mattress protectors on my side and a couple of towels under the fitted sheet. Might be a bit bulky but if my water does break during the night, I'd hate to think that it went all over and through the new mattress.

The more I think about it now, the more I'd like to try and have him as naturally as possible and maybe not even get induced. I know it's pretty much out of my hands, but I'm sort of hoping he'll make his appearance today or tomorrow. I still have a doctor's appointment tomorrow afternoon and I'm guessing there'll be an internal and we'll work out for sure what's going on from there. It's still not always real and I know the next 72 hours are going to be a spin out for everyone involved.

Sam is up here with me now, which I'm so incredibly happy about. She's so excited. It's awesome and she is keeping me excited as well. She brought up a couple of gorgeous outfits for bub which she was pretty pleased about. It was very cute.

Second last entry for Part 2

This will probably be my last entry in this diary for part 2.

I sort of feel sad now writing this, as this diary has been the place for stress relief, therapy, an outlet for so many tears, lots of smiles and has been of incredibly great comfort to me on this adventure. This is an adventure that will hopefully leave me the mother of a gorgeous little boy in less than two days' time. I look back and it's hard to believe everything we've gone through in the last two years. It has definitely brought us closer together now and I feel like our marriage is stronger than ever. I am sure this has a lot to do with how much love we both feel for our little unborn child.

I am looking forward to the many changes that will happen around here, the sounds and smells of a baby, and filling the nursery with everything that is him. I am so looking forward to holding him, cuddling him, smelling him, and telling him how much his Mummy and Daddy love him and have looked forward to meeting him for so long. I'm so much looking forward to teaching him and showing him things in life and experiencing a proper family and a normal upbringing for him.

I am looking forward to sharing and encouraging his hopes and dreams, his aspirations, his own adventures in his life and I am looking forward to introducing him to new siblings that we hope to have after him.

I am so glad I have not taken any part of this pregnancy for granted and wish everyone could feel like this in the sense that we so appreciate what we are about to receive. We truly feel so blessed in the fact that we are about to have a baby and to become parents knowing there are so many people out there that won't ever experience what we have.

I have thoroughly enjoyed the last five months or so of being pregnant when I have been able to just bask in the joy that I've felt every time he moves or kicks or pushes little feet out my side. We have already shared some special moments each night when I have held my hands on my bare belly and just felt for him. More often than not he has responded and nine times out of ten, he has said goodnight to me and I wouldn't swap this time for anything else in the world. It's been an incredibly special and very personal experience feeling him move inside me and I am so grateful that Scott has been able to get a bit of an idea of what I'm feeling inside, on the outside.

My son is going to have the very best life has to offer.

So, with that, I will sign off now. I am filled with anticipation and excitement; I have tears of joy in my eyes and so much love in my heart at the impending arrival of our beautiful first born. It is almost seventeen months to the date of my first entry and fourteen months to the date of Part II, and I will finish here. I look forward to sharing with you again writing more in the future, what we will call part three.

It looks like we made it! God only knows how!

Monday 8th July 2002

At 3:45pm we had our last appointment. I was examined and told that I was 1-2cm dilated already and that if we wanted to, we could book in to the hospital and have our baby induced that night! This would mean an approximate arrival on the Tuesday sometime between 12-3pm. That stunned both Scott and I and after we had both stopped crying, we left the decision up to the doctor. She said there was no advantage to waiting another day and it was a good idea to move while all the conditions were so perfect. We left her office a bit in shock and drove home quietly both trying to think of everything we hadn't done, as we weren't expecting to have another day.

We got home to a super excited Auntie Sam, and Scott had something to eat. I drank a cup of tea and feeling pretty nervous, overnight bag in hand; we got back in the car and drove to the hospital.

Part Three

Benjamin Sam Shaw

On the night of Monday 8th July 2002, Scott and I arrived at the hospital about 9pm. We checked in and took some time to get ourselves organised. The midwife examined me, and I was still a long way off, and only about 2cm dilated. She gave me some prostaglandin gel, a hormone that helps to get your body ready for labour and also helps to move things along a little. She also gave me a couple of sleeping tablets which I took very reluctantly and sent us to our room. We were in room twelve and it was now nearly 11pm.

I had never been one to take painkillers, even a paracetemol, except when I *really* felt I needed one. I had never had a sleeping tablet before and whilst part of me did not want to release what control I had over the next few hours, another part of me was scared after everything we had been through, that now I would miss something.

About 2am on Tuesday 9th July, I woke with the first of my contractions. The pain got gradually stronger and about 2:45am Scott rang the nurse. She checked me over and gave me two more painkilling tablets to help.

The contractions steadily increased and became more and more uncomfortable and by 6am, the pain was now intense, and we were moved to the labour ward.

After a relatively short labour by most peoples' standards, the assistance of some gas and a shot of pethidine, it was all over.

At **8:47am** our most beautiful angel Benjamin Sam Shaw, made his appearance into the world. He was truly the most gorgeous thing I had ever seen in my life. Even amidst my hazy vision and fuzzy head, I remember thinking "*he's so perfect*". Scott and I both cried and I couldn't believe we'd finally done it. The little man that had kicked inside me and I'd grown to love so much over the last nine months, was finally here. Weighing in at 7 pounds 3 ounces, 3205gm, with a head of dark curly hair, intense dark blue eyes and absolutely perfect in every way, I fell in love immediately.

I lay there with my lips to his soft head breathing in his smell and wanting to take a permanent mental snapshot of this single moment in time. Tears rolled down my cheeks and I knew it had been worth every single frustration, every single disappointment, every painful minute and I would have done it all again in a heartbeat to be back in this moment. I was completely in love.

I remember feeling stunned at everything that had happened in the last few hours and months and could hardly believe my son was actually here. He was real, and he was snuggled up in my arms. It was like watching a movie.

Over the next twenty-four hours I rarely took my eyes

off him. The tears continued to fall as I was overwhelmed with an incredibly beautiful feeling of deep love and an intense need to nurture and protect my beautiful baby boy. I had never been so incredibly happy or ever known a love like I felt for this little man. I knew instantly that things in my life would never be the same again.

Over the next few days, the emotions continued to run high and many tears were shed by both Scott and me.

The dream had come true; we had been blessed with a perfect and gorgeous baby boy.

I now had a son.

The First Two Weeks

Life would change significantly for Scott and I over the next two years starting with the first two weeks. We now had to learn how to raise our baby together and it was going to come with challenges and lessons.

I remember saying at the time, babies should be born with a manual. It should be a smooth birth where the baby comes out easily, the placenta should slip out next and the instruction manual follows last.

You would think that after everything I had been through, the next part would be easy and that was what I had expected. It was far from easy and almost from the beginning, I found myself running into problems and on more than one occasion, second guessing myself as a mother.

It all started with the breast feeding. This was not the simple exercise I had been led to believe and I had even completed the course! I had the theory and I knew what I was supposed to do. As it turned out, and a topic that was not covered in my training, my nipples were not ideal *'baby feeding nipples'*. Feeding my baby quickly turned into a nightmare and continued to deteriorate rapidly after we got home. Despite my every effort and persistence to get it right, what nipples I had had become cracked and badly damaged and this only made the situation worse. I tried all the shields and gadgets I could find on the market to make it work, but nothing seemed to help.

It became agony to feed Ben and I was hating the whole experience. This was supposed to be a wonderful bonding experience for him and I and I was breaking out in a cold sweat every time I thought of him getting close to meal time. He wasn't getting enough milk from me and I thought I was going to die, every time he tried to latch on. I was at my wits end and crying nearly constantly.

Over the course of the next two weeks, he lost weight instead of gaining it and more weight than they are supposed to lose, which naturally sent me into a panic. I was incredibly stressed and had no idea what to do.

For most of that first week home, I felt like I was floating around the house, not doing anything except feeding unsuccessfully, crying and becoming increasingly stressed. Once again, I felt like I was watching myself from outside my body and could see everything happening and was completely powerless and without the energy to do any more than I felt I already was.

I began the fight in my head as to whether to persist with breastfeeding or just switch to a bottle and formula. It hurt so much that I couldn't feed my own baby and I didn't want to stop breastfeeding but I couldn't see me continuing with the stress that I was feeling before each feed and I knew it was not about me anymore. The most important thing in the world now was what was best for Ben. This would become a theme I would follow for many years to come and would be a crucial part of every single decision I would ever make in the future.

Another day passed, and I was totally beside myself. I couldn't keep going like this for my sanity and the sanity of my husband. He was also being dragged along for the ride with me and above all I knew things had to change for the benefit of Ben.

I made a phone call and booked an appointment for the next day at a local baby clinic. After spending over an hour there and with many tears shed, Scott and I made the only decision there was to make in that moment. That day we switched to formula and began bottle feeding Ben, so we could get his weight back up to where it was supposed to be.

From that minute on, something clicked in my brain and I felt an overwhelming responsibility to Ben and to myself to prove that I was not a bad mother, like I was starting to feel like. Ben was nine days old.

Breastfeeding was one of the hardest things I'd had to do so far as a mother and I knew it would not be the last. They tell you all the theory in the classroom and during the course that I had completed. They write books, and papers on how "*breast is best*", and it is strongly encouraged but no one tells you that if you have 'less than perfect' nipples then it won't happen easily for you, if at all. Not being able to breastfeed is not always just that the baby isn't latched on properly.

The switch to formula brought on more emotional

anxiety for me and I felt like I was now only capable of washing and filling bottles and was no longer capable of even looking after my own child. It seemed Scott was a way better parent than I was, and I never felt anything other than the utmost admiration for him. Ben would settle for him and not for me. Scott could feed him, and I couldn't, as he would smell the milk on me and would not take the bottle from me.

Scott was my hero and I felt like my world was falling apart. Was everything I had worked for, for over two years and my dreams of being a wonderful mother falling apart? Everything was happening in slow motion right in front of my own eyes and I was almost paralysed.

I wrote in an email to Maria

... I'm waiting for the day when things are nice again. When Ben is feeding happily every time on the bottle, when I don't cry every day and when I can get through the day without physical pain in my breasts, without milk wet t-shirts and without this pain in my heart that won't subside.

In such a short time, I had made myself sick with tears again and had convinced myself that I was not cut out for motherhood. The dream that I'd always wanted was shattering. I was feeling incapable of doing the most basic thing for my child. My thoughts spiralled out of control and I had moments where I felt that I couldn't do anything right and was hurting so badly emotionally, that I couldn't even think straight.

There were moments I felt so shattered, heartbroken and devastated. I couldn't help feeling ripped off again and wondered what if I was not actually cut out for motherhood after all? Could that even be a possibility I had not previously considered in my entire baby planning? I mean, surely every mother can feed her own child, right?

My tears continued to flow for what seemed forever and this put added strain on Scott and me during an already difficult time. I cannot begin to explain how devastating this period felt for me. I look back now and what seemed like a deal breaker for me at the time is so obvious to me today. I clearly just needed some help! I probably also had a good dose of *baby blues* or perhaps even a bit of post-natal depression. My hormones would have been all over the place and I just couldn't see the forest for the trees.

Over the following week or two things did settle down and I wrote:

I think back now that I'm feeling better and getting some sleep and don't know how I got through these last weeks. I don't ever want to be in this place again, yet I know that with baby number two I probably will be. This time will be worse as I'll have a toddler too. Maybe it will be better though because I will have the benefit of experience under my belt.

I know that I can't do it alone though and have a whole new respect for single mothers. I know that Scott is stronger than I ever could have imagined and has taken to his new role of Daddy like a duck to water. He fits right in and is so wonderful with Ben. He dotes on him and looks at him adoringly. I sometimes feel that he makes a better father than I do a mother, but I guess it's just my perception of what it seems like after a hellish start to motherhood.

About three weeks later things changed again, and in

another direction for me. I was aware one afternoon; I had little wet patches on my bra where I must have leaked a tiny bit during the day. It took me completely by surprise as I thought that my milk had dried up for good and in my fog, I had not noticed this before now. I wondered if it was possible I was being given a second chance?

After a few phone calls and a lot of online research I discovered there was something called Re Lactation. Why did I not know about this concept previously? Why had no one told me? This information reignited a spark in me and filled me with an incredible sense of excitement and determination and I knew I had to give it a go! I was well aware it was a long shot and the nurses also confirmed this, but I knew I had to at least try. A part of me was positive I would make it happen and I was prepared to do whatever it took.

The next day equipped with some tools, I began a process of expressing milk around the clock every three hours for anywhere up to an hour at a time and once again, that obsessive compulsion to succeed took over in me. I started with just a few millilitres at a time but slowly and surely my milk supply continued to gradually increase.

Scott was pretty much against the whole idea from the beginning as he had seen me nearly hysterical last time and didn't want me, or him, to go through this all over again. His thought process was, Ben is now putting on weight, he is happy with the formula, it is not broken any more why are you trying to fix it? I couldn't explain it to him. I knew he wouldn't understand and this was the cause of many a 'discussion' between us.

Over the next few weeks, I poured my heart and soul into making this work. I had to do whatever it took; I had to prove to myself and on some level prove to Ben, that not only was I a great mother, but I could also feed my child as well.

I booked in and attended a local clinic every day for a week. Here I met an incredible nurse, who to this day I shall be forever grateful. She absolutely changed my life. She taught me some amazing things, some do's and don'ts and armed me with vitamins, milk increasing tablets, and a whole pile of information. My mission had begun.

I had also sourced a naturopath and began drinking the most disgusting but effective concoction I had ever come across, called Chicken Essence. It was used at the time for many ailments in the world of naturopathy including the increasing of breast milk whilst adding richness to the milk that was produced.

The Naturopath was very clear about how to make sure I swallowed this liquid and advised me to hold my nose and just gulp down the small bottle of drink as fast as possible like a shot. He advised to follow it immediately with a glass of water or juice and eat something sweet straight afterwards to complete this three-step process. His words were that I did not *ever* want to taste it as I would not keep it down. I started with two - three jars a day and at $3 a jar there was no way I was not keeping it down! It was another small price to pay and after a short while, I knew it was working.

Everything I did was for Ben and all with very deliberate actions. I have to say here, it also went against the advice of many well-meaning people I spoke with, both friends and professionals. My stubborn personality and pig-headed persistence was not letting go of this and I was determined to succeed. This *would* work!

By the end of August, not even six weeks after he was born, I was completely breastfeeding Ben and very successfully. There was no more breast damage, and he was consistently gaining weight. Mummy was delighted, and baby was happy too. There was no more formula.

Did I feel proud of myself? Hell yeah!! The feeling was incredible! I WAS a good mother after all!!

The Next Chapter

One of the reasons I include the previous story in this book, is I know that my perception at the beginning of this journey, was that the IVF was going to be the hardest part, and in a lot of circumstances it was. The IVF was just the beginning though. I did not anticipate what would come after he was born and how it would make me question a lot of what I had believed up until that point.

I always knew in the back of my mind, there was the possibility of a difficult birth, but I had never been too concerned with that, and would take it as it came. I had assumed everything after that should be reasonably simple. I was not naive in thinking it would all be 'perfect and smooth sailing', but I was not prepared for how confronting and painful this next experience would be, and how it would rock me to the very core as a mother and as a woman. I could not have known at the time that everything that had happened from the planning and the conception to the birth and those first two weeks would begin to mould me into the type of mother I was to become.

Perhaps it is just my personality or my stubbornness and passion for success once I put my mind to something, I don't know. I can't honestly say that every part of me knew for sure it was even going to work, but that didn't matter, a strong and defiant part of me did. What I knew for sure was I had to give it everything I had. It was too important to me. Ben was too important to me and I wouldn't give up until I absolutely had to.

I look back on my life, and the IVF journey and the feeding experience both impacted me more than I initially realised. These challenges absolutely contributed to who I am today, and there have been numerous decisions I have made since then to '*make it work at all costs*'. I grin as I write this, as not all my endeavours have been as successful, and I have not always recognised when to give up.

I read a book once and it talked about '*seeing the writing on the wall, acknowledging it, and doing something about it*'. I have many a time, seen the writing on the wall... and kept going down my current path anyway. Whilst I have no regrets about anything in my life, I now understand that sometimes I just have to '*let it go*'. I am a work in progress...

In May of 2003, we started trying for baby number two and three and underwent our third full round of IVF. Ben was now ten months old and I had the urgent feeling again that I wanted a sibling for him and I wanted to continue to grow our family. Over the next eighteen months we completed a further three full rounds of IVF and each round came with a new set of challenges and scenarios.

By the last two rounds, I was giving my own injections, and trying to keep Scott out of the emotional process as much as possible. With each month, came the same, if not steeper and more emotional roller coaster for me. At times I felt like I was again completely losing my mind. My frustration increased as did my impatience as I knew I had succeeded once, so theoretically it *could* happen again. It was not impossible, but the wait was making me crazy. I was also very aware of my biological clock ticking louder and louder as each try failed and my sense of urgency growing stronger each month that passed.

During this time, we experienced a round where we had fourteen eggs and only one fertilised and that in itself they said was a miracle. We experienced a round where we had fifteen eggs and no viable sperm to fertilise any of them. There were many other scenarios and let downs and it was a completely mental time in my life.

Many years later I would use the analogy of a gambler playing a slot machine. The thought process for me was the same. If I just kept trying, eventually I had to have a win, right? It was just a matter of time?

Surely it was just a matter of me not giving up? I had won before, so it was possible to win again.

In total, between March 2000 and March 2005 Scott and I underwent 6 full IVF cycles. This included a full round of drugs each time. At least 84 eggs were collected, 34 fertilised, 25 frozen and I had 8 transfers performed comprising of a combination of fresh and frozen embryos. I had one miscarriage and we were blessed with one beautifully perfect baby boy.

These numbers do not include the four artificial inseminations and the numerous months we tried from April 1999 to conceive naturally without assistance. This period of time cost us nearly $50,000.

When Scott and I first commenced our baby making exercise we were warned, and it was brought to our attention on more than one occasion the impact this process could have on our relationship and our marriage. We went into this with our eyes wide open, but we could never have been prepared for the emotional roller coaster we would embark on for the next four-year period.

There are times during this story, looking back, where it was obvious from what I wrote that an increasingly amount of pressure was being placed on our marriage and I guess if I am honest, I was becoming somewhat obsessed and completely consumed with having a baby, or several babies at any cost. As happens so often during this process, somewhere along the way Scott and I as a couple got lost. I know whilst he initially wanted more than one child, after what we went through to have Ben I knew one would be enough for him. It just wasn't enough for me and I paid a high price for this.

Incredibly our last attempt to have another child together was in March 2005. I know this was purely my decision and not a joint decision. I just didn't want to acknowledge the writing on the wall and was grasping for whatever I could in a sad and final attempt to satisfy what seemed to be an overwhelming need for me to have more children. We separated just two months later in May.

The Final Rides

I wish I could say this is where it ended, and I got over it and moved on, but it wasn't. A lot of what I was feeling at the time and what Scott was feeling was never documented here, but suffice to say, over time our connection was lost.

I should make something very clear at this point, whilst our separation was not *solely* due to the pressures of trying to have a family and there was a lot more going on than that, I have no doubt the added stress this put on our relationship did not help us. My obsession or determination to fulfil what I so desperately wanted in having a family certainly didn't help either. At the time, I just couldn't be completely happy with what I had and knowing and experiencing how wonderful our gorgeous son was, I wanted more. Nothing else would satisfy me.

After our split, I kept a fairly low profile and my life continued to be all about Ben. I was now back working part time and trying to come to terms with my marriage breakdown and the impact it would have on my son and the decision was made to put our dream home on the market. In March 2006 I bought a small house and Ben and I moved into it. He was nearly four years old and it was now just the two of us.

My mind was now consumed with what I had done to Ben and if he would be okay as a result of his dad and I no longer being together. Scott remained, and still plays a very active part in his life and sees him several times a week. I think it was as hard on him at the time, not living with Ben full time any more, as it was for me wondering what damage I had potentially done to Ben that he hadn't asked for.

In 2006, almost a year after Scott and I had separated, I went out for drinks with some friends, and I had a one-night stand, something extremely out of character for me. Unfortunately, the condom broke during the evening, something I had only ever heard about, but wondered how and if it could actually happen. I acknowledged what had happened at the time, but didn't think too much more of it, and life went on as usual. As luck would have it, I met a great guy within the next few days, who happened to have two beautiful boys of his own, and we started seeing each other. About three weeks later, it occurred to me I had not had a period in a while and to my disbelief, I realised I was in fact pregnant.

Words cannot even begin to describe how I was feeling. To say I was stunned was a huge understatement. Here I was, I had just moved into a new house and was starting out in a brand-new relationship, and now discovered after years of trying and so much energy poured into having my gorgeous son, that I was pregnant to a guy I had only known for a few hours in one night. Having read my story so far can you even begin to imagine where I was in my head? I was spinning out of control and completely torn. What was I supposed to do? Getting rid of it was definitely not an option and telling the guy in question wasn't either. We had had no contact since that night and I only knew he lived interstate. I saw my only option being raising this baby on my own and working it out as I went along. I was both terrified and exhilarated at the same time.

As it sometimes happens, my mouth engaged before my brain had a chance to catch up and I had a very awkward conversation with my new partner. I fully expected him to walk away and said I wouldn't blame him if he did and I was okay with whatever he decided. His response took me completely by surprise and without missing a beat said, "*okay, we will raise it as our own*".

Floored once again!! Who says that to a woman they have just met? Who tells that to a guy she has just met? Who does this happen to? What the hell was going on? Was this seriously happening? I had so many questions.

Within the next day or so I decided I better have a blood test to confirm and the test revealed the levels were lower than they should have been. I knew instantly what this meant; I *had* been pregnant... but was no longer.

Once again, I was taken by a huge force and shaken to my core. It had opened up a Pandora's Box I was not expecting at this point in my life and now had no idea what to do about it.

This of course prompted many conversations over the next few weeks as to what we both wanted out of life and our futures. There were several occasions where I made it quite clear I wanted to have more children and it *was* a deal breaker for me. To put it bluntly, if this was not in his plan then there was no point continuing this relationship. He then told me he had had a vasectomy and having more children was not an option. It nearly broke us up. I am not sure why it didn't.

We did stay together, and as our relationship grew stronger and we moved in together, so did my obsession and determination to have another baby. I rang my trusty gynaecologist/obstetrician and made an appointment to investigate the options. I was determined there had to be a way around this.

As it turned out, there was a process called aspiration, which involved him going under anaesthetic and having sperm surgically removed. I thought "*we could do that*", then use these sperm to fertilise some of the eggs I still had frozen or of course, do a full round of IVF and use fresh eggs.

The next two years were ridiculous for us and our blended family. Ben was now five years old, and his boys were nine and eleven. After thawing all nine eggs I still had frozen, only one fertilised. Clearly this was not going to work. Our only other option was to try again with a full IVF cycle or go down the track of donor sperm. He seemed totally fine with this idea and had grown excited at the prospect of us having a baby together to complement our other three boys. This of course would be my dream come true and complete my family of four children. Perfect. Once again, I accepted the mental mission and was ready to go.

So, we made a decision and decided to give the donor sperm option a go. This was a bizarre experience and much like interviewing candidates you never meet for a job. We were given a pile of resume style documents of various donors based on a few criteria we had chosen. I can't remember why, and what the information was we had at the time, but the decision was made to use imported sperm from the USA. We felt this was the better option and would give us more chances of success. We read up on the process and out of the 'resumes', we picked our donor.

In a very surreal experience some time later, we happened to be watching an interview on a current affairs program with an American male who had donated his sperm. I got goose bumps all over as I stared at the man on the TV screen in disbelief. His description and answers to their questions matched what I had read on his 'resume' 100%. I knew for sure that this was the same donor we had chosen, and I was now seeing and hearing him on the screen in my lounge room. It was like something from out of this world.

Over the next eighteen months we completed numerous artificial inseminations by donor (AID) procedures, all of which were unsuccessful. I started to realise now that it was possibly a problem on my part and even the best quality sperm was not going to cut it. By this stage I was 37 years old and my biological clock was ticking louder and louder as each month went by.

In February 2008 at 38 years old I underwent my seventh and last IVF cycle. Eight eggs were harvested and four were fertilised with donor sperm. Two embryos were transferred to me. I did not fall pregnant.

It took me a long time after that to come to terms with the fact that I would never have a blood sibling for Ben. A part of me felt I had let him down in some way, knowing he would never have lots of brothers and sisters to grow up with, to play with and to learn from. It broke my heart. I had never wanted him to be an only child and despite having two extra children in my new relationship, anyone that has a blended family, knows at the end of the day, no matter how you feel about them, they are never really yours.

I would look at people around me having babies including teachers when Ben started school and without exception it would bring tears to my eyes. I quietly mourned what would never be, and at times, thought the pain would never ever go away. I couldn't seem to get over it and couldn't bring myself to accept it was over.

It was as painful as when Scott and I had first started the journey and getting news of friends falling pregnant. I did my best to try and mean that I was 'so very happy' for them but inside I was crying. Sometimes I didn't feel like I meant my well wishes at all. I was once again filled with feelings of envy and resentment. *'Why aren't I pregnant?'*, *'why are you pregnant?'* I mentally questioned those that I felt didn't *'deserve'* to be pregnant and it was a painful and intense feeling.

As time went by, I eventually did accept what was

happening and life went on. I realised that I had been playing the illusive slot machine, and it was now time to stop. It was time to stop trying to achieve something that was clearly not going to happen no matter what I did, or how much I wanted it. It just wasn't meant to be, and I couldn't fix this. I had absolutely no control over what was happening, and for me this was once again a devastating feeling.

I had always been able to fix things! I had always been able to make things happen, but this was beyond even my capabilities.

I remember thinking sometime after my blended relationship came to a very ugly end in 2013, and he moved interstate, that I would have been left raising a five-year-old. The baby would have been donor sperm and knowing his state of mind at the time when he left, I have no doubt he would have had no further involvement in this child's life and raising two children on my own would have more than likely been the outcome.

I have always believed things happen for a reason, and in that moment, I felt a wave of gratitude and finally an understanding of why I had not been successful in my attempts for a second baby.

Right from the beginning and through all of this, in some weird way, the whole experience had continued to strengthen the bond between Ben and I and we had grown and continued to grow fiercely close. Even though I had been in a relationship, there was always an underlying sense of it was always me and him. We were a team, we were buddies and we had so much fun together. As I moved through the acceptance of knowing it would just be the two of us from then on, I became incredibly grateful once again for what I had and what we had together and as always, he continued to be my number one priority.

As the years have gone by, I did completely get over my desire for more children and stopped thinking about what could have been.

Today, I have the most incredible relationship with my son and Scott and I remain very close. He is still extremely active in Ben's life and for his sake we have always had an openly amicable relationship, even in the beginning of our separation when things were at their most strained.

We have often had the conversation about why parents that separate feel the need to run down the other partner. We have never done this, and I guess Ben has truly always and very deliberately come first.

Scott, his girlfriend, and I, have a special relationship and most people from the outside looking in find it very unusual. For us it is normal, and it works.

As Ben grows up, he has not been affected by not having permanent siblings around and he did learn a lot from his 'temporary brothers' during the five years my ex and I were together.

I believe we prioritise and make time for what is most important to us in each moment in our lives. Relationships are the same and we have to take very deliberate actions. Maintaining them is not always easy as life circumstances change and people themselves change and grow. I am a firm believer and can prove however, that it can be done with very deliberate and mindful actions.

If I could write a list of wishes of how I would want my relationship with my son to be, I can honestly say I would not change a single thing.

We have been through some stuff together and are not only mother and son but very close friends. We confide in each other and have always had a unique closeness as well as a high respect for each other and our decisions and opinions.

In the first few pages of this book, I wrote:

I wanted to grow someone up, who I could teach and learn from at the same time... and we would have wonderful experiences and would travel the world, and that I would work hard to have an amazing relationship with... and that they would never ever want for anything.

There is not a day that goes by that I do not feel grateful, as I have all of this. Ben and I have had some amazing experiences and have travelled together, to Canada, Fiji and Israel, and there are more adventures on the cards. I have learnt so much from my son already and I continue to learn from him every single day.

In a conversation recently, I asked him if he had a million dollars in his pocket what would he buy. He replied without batting an eyelid "*Mum there's nothing I want. I have everything I want...*"

So... You want to have a baby? And it's making you feel crazy?

I absolutely get it! I felt *exactly* the same way...

P.S.

So, you may ask, is this where it ends? Is this the end of the story? Is it finished now? Is it done?

I can honestly answer all those questions with tears in my eyes and a definite "No".

It has only just begun...

About The Author

Born in the UK and living most of her life in Australia, author Dalya Shaw is passionate about life and love. People who meet her are greeted by her warm and infectious bubbly personality.

She is no stranger to traumatic endings but also considers herself blessed with wonderful beginnings. Ever since she can remember, she had dreamed about having a wonderful and beautiful family with three or four children of her own.

In It's Okay to Feel Crazy Trying to Have a Baby, Dalya documents her journey of trying to create that special family. As she narrates the story of her invitro fertilization treatment in a diary beginning in 2001, she takes you through the exhilarating highs and devastating lows of her treatment.

Spanning eight years this memoir gives insight into both the physical and emotional effects of trying to become pregnant.

Real and raw, It's Okay to Feel Crazy Trying to Have a Baby reinforces Dalya's determination to become a great mother. Her story serves to inspire others and it offers hope and encouragement to those facing similar challenges.

Printed in the United States
By Bookmasters